Communicating & Connecting With Social Media

WILLIAM M. FERRITER

JASON T. RAMSDEN

ERIC C. SHENINGER

A Joint Publication

555 North Morton Street
Bloomington, IN 47404
800.733.6786 (toll free) / 812.336.7700
FAX: 812.336.7790

email: info@solution-tree.com
solution-tree.com

Visit **go.solution-tree.com/technology** to download the reproducibles in this book.

Printed in the United States of America

15 14 13 12 11   1 2 3 4 5

FSC
Mixed Sources
Product group from well-managed
forests and other controlled sources

Cert no. SW-COC-002283
www.fsc.org
© 1996 Forest Stewardship Council

Library of Congress Cataloging-in-Publication Data

Ferriter, William M.

Communicating and connecting with social media / William M. Ferriter, Jason T. Ramsden, Eric C. Sheninger.

p. cm.

Includes bibliographical references and index.

ISBN 978-1-935249-54-2 (perfect bound) -- ISBN 978-1-935249-53-5 (library edition) 1. Mass media in education--United States. 2. Media literacy--Study and teaching (Secondary)--United States. 3. Popular culture--Study and teaching (Secondary)--United States. I. Ramsden, Jason T. II. Sheninger, Eric C. III. Title.

LB1043.F47 2011

371.33'3--dc22

2011010101

Solution Tree
Jeffrey C. Jones, CEO & President

Solution Tree Press
President: Douglas M. Rife
Publisher: Robert D. Clouse
Vice President of Production: Gretchen Knapp
Managing Production Editor: Caroline Wise
Copy Editor: Sarah Payne-Mills
Proofreader: Tara Perkins
Text Designer: Jenn Taylor
Cover Designer: Orlando Angel

To my beautiful wife Elizabeth, who Reece and I just couldn't live without! —Bill Ferriter

To Colleen—my wife, best friend, and colleague—whose unwavering love and incredible support I am blessed to have in all facets of my life. And to my children, Connor and Kaitlin, who keep me smiling and laughing every day. —Jason Ramsden

To my incredible wife Melissa, a phenomenal mother to Nicholas and Isabella, my confidant and best friend, whose love and support I treasure. —Eric Sheninger

ACKNOWLEDGMENTS

Like all pieces of writing, *Communicating and Connecting With Social Media* is the product of a thousand conversations and shared experiences. For Bill, those conversations have happened almost exclusively online—in digital places like the comment sections of Scott McLeod's and Dean Shareski's blogs and in the Twitter streams of folks like Russ Goerend, Steven Anderson, and Jon Becker. People he's never met like Chris Wejr, Lyn Hilt, and Eric Townsley have shaped his thinking—pushing, prodding, encouraging, and contradicting. Their contributions—and the contributions of hundreds of others who have embraced the notion that transparent sharing can make everyone better—are a constant source of ideas and inspiration for Bill.

For Jason, those conversations began in February 2008 with friend and likeminded soul Matt Scully during the National Association of Independent Schools' annual conference where keynotes by Daniel Pink and Sir Ken Robinson helped to fundamentally shift his mindset about education. Since then, those conversations have continued, both on and offline, and have grown to include trusted friends and thinkers Sam Morris, Sarah Hanawald, and Meredith Stewart—and countless others in his personal learning network, including Jonathan E. Martin and Jamie Field Baker—each challenging Jason in ways he previously thought not possible. Lastly, Jason wishes to thank Doreen Kelly whose support and encouragement has been invaluable throughout this career.

For Eric, those conversations began in March 2009 when he joined Twitter and began to craft his personal learning network. There he came across a wide array of passionate educators like Thomas Whitby and Pam Moran. Principals like Patrick Larkin, George Couros, Chris Lehmann, and Deron Durflinger whose support, guidance, and unwavering commitment to share their knowledge have helped transform him into the leader that he is today. Eric would be remiss if he did not mention the New Milford High School community—students, staff, administrators, and parents—who collectively inspire him each day to continually grow and lead change in way that makes his school the best it can be.

Finally, Bill, Jason, and Eric would like to thank the staff of Solution Tree. Sarah Payne-Mills has helped to shepherd the book from a rough first draft to a much improved final copy, with insight and encouragement every step of the way. Gretchen Knapp has served as a constant sounding board, providing support even when we were overwhelmed, and Douglas Rife and Diana Brace sought out the feedback needed to ensure that the ideas shared within this text carried resonance with leaders in the integration of social media in schools.

Solution Tree Press would like to thank the following reviewers:

Shadow William Jon Armfield
Assistant Professor, Department of
  Educational Technology
Northern Arizona University
Flagstaff, Arizona

Grant Foster
Principal
Bethel Elementary School
Salem, Oregon

Brent Gaswick
Technology Integration Specialist
Nebraska Department of Education
Lincoln, Nebraska

Elizabeth Ross Hubbell
Lead Consultant
McREL
Denver, Colorado

Laurie Keating
Vice President
Technology Planning and Organizational
  Development Center for Education,
  Leadership, and Technology
Marlborough, Massachusetts

Matthew Levinson
Head of the Middle School
The Nueva School
Hillsborough, California

Pam Petersen
Eighth-Grade Science Teacher
York Middle School
York, Nebraska

Lisa Sjogren
Technology Integration Collaborative Teacher
Osseo Area Schools ISD #279
Maple Grove, Minnesota

Laura Zieger
Associate Professor, Department of
  Educational Technology
New Jersey City University
Jersey City, New Jersey

TABLE OF CONTENTS

Reproducible pages are in italics.
Visit **go.solution-tree.com/technology** to download the reproducibles in this book.

2

ABOUT THE AUTHORS

William M. Ferriter—@plugusin on Twitter—is a sixth-grade teacher in a professional learning community (PLC) near Raleigh, North Carolina. A National Board Certified Teacher, Bill has designed professional development courses for educators nationwide. His trainings include how to use blogs, wikis, and podcasts in the classroom; the role of iTunes in teaching and learning; and the power of digital moviemaking. Bill has also developed schoolwide technology rubrics and surveys that identify student and staff digital proficiency at the building level. He is a founding member and senior fellow of the Teacher Leaders Network and has served as teacher in residence at the Center for Teaching Quality.

An advocate for PLCs, improved teacher working conditions, and teacher leadership, Bill has represented educators on Capitol Hill and presented at state and national conferences. He is among the first one hundred teachers in North Carolina and the first one thousand in the United States to earn certification from the National Board for Professional Teaching Standards. He has been a Regional Teacher of the Year in North Carolina, and his blog, the Tempered Radical, earned Best Teacher Blog of 2008 from Edublogs. Bill has had articles published in the *Journal of Staff Development, Educational Leadership,* and *Threshold Magazine.*

A contributing author to two assessment anthologies, *The Teacher as Assessment Leader* and *The Principal as Assessment Leader,* he is also coauthor of *Teaching the iGeneration* and *Building a Professional Learning Community at Work*™, Learning Forward's (formerly National Staff Development Council) 2010 Professional Development Book of the Year. Bill earned a bachelor of science and master of science in elementary education from the State University of New York at Geneseo. To learn more about Bill's work, visit http://bit.ly/temperedradical.

Jason T. Ramsden—@raventech on Twitter—is the chief technology officer for Ravenscroft School in Raleigh, North Carolina. He has taught and coached in independent middle and high schools since 1991, has been involved in admissions and school communications, and has been an advocate for using instructional technology to help improve teaching and learning since his first appointment as a director of technology in 1997.

Presently, Jason serves as chair of the North Carolina Association of Independent Schools' Commission on Technology and writes for its blog Igniting Innovation. He is a member of the National Association of

Independent Schools' 21st Century Curriculum/Technology Task Force and a member of the Consortium of School Networking Chief Technology Officers' advisory council. A national presenter on school communication and innovation, he has twice presented at the annual CASE-NAIS Independent Schools Conference, where in 2010 he received the Faculty Star Award. He has also presented at National Association of Independent Schools' annual conference as well as at the inaugural Education Innovation Summit. Prior to his appointment to Ravenscroft, Jason served as technology manager at the Hill Center in Durham, North Carolina; network administrator and technical support manager at Convent of the Sacred Heart in Greenwich, Connecticut; director of technology at Trinity-Pawling School in Pawling, New York; associate director of admissions at Trinity-Pawling School; and director of admissions and public relations at Xavier High School in New York City.

Jason holds a master of science in education, administration, and supervision from Fordham University in New York and a bachelor of arts in psychology from Loyola College in Maryland. To learn more about Jason's work, visit www.jasonramsden.com.

Eric C. Sheninger—@NMHS_Principal on Twitter—is the principal at New Milford High School in Bergen County, New Jersey. He is passionate about establishing and fostering learning environments that are student centered, collaborative, flexible, and capable of preparing all learners to succeed in the 21st century.

As an educational administrator, he firmly believes that effective communication, listening, support, shared decision making, and the integration of technology are essential elements necessary for the transformation of school cultures. Eric has emerged as an innovative leader in the use of social media and web 2.0 technology as tools to engage students, improve communications with stakeholders, and help educators grow professionally. Eric is a Google Certified Teacher and an ASCD 2011 Conference Scholar. He was also named to the National School Boards Association "20 to Watch" list in 2010 for technology leadership. He now presents and speaks nationally, assisting other school leaders who are working to embrace and effectively utilize technology. His blog, A Principal's Reflections, earned first runner-up in the Best Administrator Blog category in 2010 from Edublogs.

Eric began his career in education as a science teacher and coach at Watchung Hills Regional High School in Warren, New Jersey. He then transitioned into the field of educational administration as an athletic director and supervisor of physical education and health and as vice principal in the New Milford School District. During his administrative career, he has served as district affirmative action officer and is the current president of the New Milford Administrators' Association. Eric earned a bachelor of science from Salisbury University, a bachelor of science from the University of Maryland Eastern Shore, and a master of education in educational administration from East Stroudsburg University. To learn more about Eric's work, visit http://ericsheninger.com.

To book Bill, Jason, or Eric for professional development, contact pd@solution-tree.com.

INTRODUCTION

Spend any time next to the water cooler in most faculty lounges, and you are bound to hear tons of interesting conversations about the role that technology is playing in our schools. Strange new phrases like "I had my students use VoiceThread to give peers feedback on their Animotos" or "Our class wiki is full of interesting poetry this year" hint at the changing nature of teaching and learning in today's classrooms. Probe a little deeper, and you will find teachers detailing their efforts to connect their classes with partners in other countries, to record tutorials for remediation and enrichment, and to improve their formative assessment practices using digital tools. While we are admittedly struggling to keep up with the rapid changes in today's new learning ecology, we are almost always collectively imagining, discussing, and debating what the classrooms of tomorrow should look like.

What you are less likely to hear are meaningful conversations about the role that social media tools—digital applications that make sharing with others easier—should play in schools. Despite having elbowed their way into our spare moments away from school—61 percent of all adults report spending at least six hours a month keeping up with friends and neighbors in digital spaces (Madden, 2010; Nielsenwire, 2010)—social media tools are generally met with skepticism and doubt from educators. "I don't see any benefit for the use of Facebook, Twitter, or any other social media in schools. . . . It's a total distraction with no benefit to learning," wrote one respondent to a survey asking for feedback on the role that social media should play in education (as cited in Ferriter, 2011b). "If the principal has time to maintain Twitter or Facebook, then they have too damn much time on their hands," wrote another (as cited in Ferriter, 2011a).

Worse yet, this skepticism often translates into policies that actively discourage educators from experimenting with social media spaces. According to *Web 2.0 in Schools: Policy and Leadership*, a joint project between the Consortium for School Networking (CoSN) and the McArthur Foundation, while 77 percent of school district leaders agreed that web 2.0 tools can lend value to teaching and learning, 70 percent currently ban social networking in their districts. As Associate Editor Meris Stansbury explained while summarizing the CoSN study for eSchool News, "Few [districts] have systemically begun to research, plan, or implement effective uses of Web 2.0 applications, nor have they restructured their schools to enable participatory reform" (Stansbury, 2010).

Our hesitance to explore the potential that social media spaces hold for schools, however, means that we are quickly being left behind by *almost everyone*. To better understand just how important social media tools are becoming, consider the following.

- Facebook—by far the largest social media destination on the web—has over 500 million users, including 69 percent of the online population in the United States and 62 percent of the online population in Canada ("Statistics," n.d.; Lenhart, Purcell, Smith, & Zickuhr, 2010).

- Over half of all Facebook users log in to the site every day, spending an average of fifty-five minutes per visit ("Statistics," n.d.; Digital Buzz Blog, 2010a).

- By the fall of 2010, Facebook had eclipsed Google in terms of web traffic, accounting for one out of every four Internet page views in the United States—the equivalent of 10 percent of all Internet traffic worldwide (Dougherty, 2010).

- With 145 million users, Twitter—a microblogging site that enables users to post and follow short, public messages online—had become the tenth-most-popular web destination in the world by the fall of 2010 (Digital Buzz Blog, 2010b; Compete, 2011; Alexa, n.d.).

- Twitter users send 50 million messages a day. That is an astonishing 600 messages per *second* (Weil, 2010).

- Perhaps most importantly for school leaders, almost 50 percent of all American Twitter users have elementary, middle, or high school–aged children (Digital Buzz Blog, 2010b).

What can we learn from these statistics? To put it simply, services like Twitter and Facebook are capturing the minds and the hearts of a social generation. Driven by the desire to connect, everyone from tweens to moms and religious leaders to politicians are arguing, debating, and creating shared knowledge together in social media spaces—and they are almost always coming back for more.

Services like Twitter and Facebook have also captured the attention of businesses and colleges, which recognize that the communication patterns of the average digital citizen are changing. Consider that 60 percent of Fortune 1000 companies are using social media tools to build vibrant communities with their clients (Ginsburg, 2010), and that 95 percent of all colleges have a strategy for using social media to stay connected with both current and prospective students (Ganim Barnes & Mattson, 2009).

For businesses and universities, social media spaces are logical extensions of traditional efforts to reach out to *customers.* In competition with other providers offering similar products or services, active social media programs gain invaluable impressions. What's more, the two-way nature of communication in social media spaces creates valuable feedback loops that can inform product development and build brand loyalty (Ginsburg, 2010). By joining conversations with target audiences, showing honesty and a willingness to listen to concerns, and energizing a core group of motivated followers, savvy businesses and universities are becoming more than cold and distant institutions to their customers. They are becoming trusted friends (Li & Bernoff, 2008).

Our central assertion in *Communicating and Connecting With Social Media* is that schools cannot continue to overlook the potential benefits that social media spaces hold for reaching out to our communities, preparing our teachers, and connecting with our kids. In this short text, we specifically examine how enterprising schools (including our own) are using social media tools to provide customized professional development for teachers. We also explore the marketing and communications value of developing a social-networking presence and examine the kinds of school and district practices necessary for supporting successful social media efforts.

We have chosen to focus on communication and professional development because schools can start using social media in those areas without violating current district policies about networking with students beyond the school day. It is our hope, however, that educators will use what they learn here about social media tools to transform their instructional practices as well.

Chapter Overviews

There is no one right way to read *Communicating and Connecting With Social Media.* If the idea of using social media spaces for communication and professional development is new to you, consider starting with chapter 1 and working your way through the entire book to gain a complete overview of what is possible. For readers already experimenting in social media spaces, however, selecting individual chapters that offer timely and appropriate advice may be a more productive strategy than tackling the text in its entirety.

To help you decide on the right strategy for reading, here are overviews of the four chapters.

Using Social Media Tools to Enhance School Communication Plans

Successful principals have always built highly functioning learning communities by clearly and consistently articulating a school's vision for—and commitment to—student success. Principals who are master communicators constantly empower teachers, keep stakeholders informed, foster relationships, and establish innovative learning cultures. Social media spaces do nothing more than make it easier for innovative principals to tackle these practices. This chapter explains several ways that administrators can use social media spaces to communicate with staff, students, parents, alumni, and other stakeholders. Strategies for improving public relations, building mutually beneficial partnerships, sharing student and teacher accomplishments, and infusing branding principles are discussed.

Using Social Media Tools to Enhance Professional Development

Professional development—particularly on the changing nature of teaching and learning in a digitally connected world—is essential as we rethink what it means to be literate in today's world. Unfortunately, many technology-related projects fail in schools due to poorly constructed learning opportunities for teachers and administrators. This chapter focuses on how administrators can structure practical, meaningful, and engaging professional development sessions on social media. Personal learning networks (PLNs) are introduced as powerful tools that educators can take advantage of in order to develop firsthand experiences with the role that social media is playing in the lives of digital learners.

Developing Professionally Responsible Social Media Practices

Social media spaces have blurred the personal and professional boundaries of educators like never before. Yet despite the well-reported implications of students' and educators' poor usage, schools and districts can implement sets of best practices to guide the proper use of these tools in education. This chapter explores the kinds of core behaviors that can help to ensure the responsible use of social media in schools.

The Future of Social Media in Education

At present, the largest segment of the population interacting in social media spaces are adults aged eighteen to twenty-nine years old. However, as generations of these connected youth become connected adults with children of their own in our schools, the future of social media in education will need to be one where schools are authentic, transparent, and consistent in their communication with stakeholders. In this final chapter, we'll examine one principal's approach to using social media today and explore how social media may change the classrooms of tomorrow.

At the end of each chapter, you will find a collection of handouts that can help to structure your work in social media spaces. This collection includes rubrics for assessing your current communication efforts, surveys for gathering feedback from the communities that you serve, tracking documents that can be used to spotlight the learning that you are doing in online spaces, and sets of suggested starting points for educators interested in building their own personal learning networks. Interactive copies of each handout can be found online at **go.solution-tree .com/technology**, the landing page for all technology-related Solution Tree titles.

Regardless of how you approach this text, it is our hope that you will begin thinking about social media spaces differently. As digital learning expert Steve Hargadon argues:

> Just as you can build either a casino or a school with basic construction materials, the materials are not the issue. It's the end use for which they are assembled and fitted. The first sites that were constructed using Web 2.0 building blocks were, as often as not, "casino-like," leading to the impression that social networking was a time waster at best, and an unsafe place to be at worst.
>
> But there's no reason why the same building blocks that built those social networking "casinos" can't be used to create schools, libraries, meeting halls, teachers' lounges—which is exactly what we're starting to see happening today. It's even arguable that these building blocks are more effective as educational tools than as social ones. (Hargadon, 2009, p. 2)

Combine the practical knowledge and tools included in this book with a bit of digital moxie, and you can fulfill Hargadon's vision of a world where social media spaces create and enhance positive learning for the teachers and the students in your schools and communities.

Using Social Media Tools to Enhance School Communication Plans

Coauthor Eric Sheninger, principal of New Milford High School in New Milford, New Jersey, believes that effective leadership begins and ends with effective communication. He argues, "If we're going to succeed as a school, I've got to get several different stakeholder groups—parents, students, community leaders, and businesses—to buy into a set of core beliefs. That means I'm constantly trying to craft messages that have resonance and trying to deliver those messages in ways that are likely to be heard. In a lot of ways, communication is the most important thing I do every day" (Sheninger, 2010a).

Researchers studying school leadership would agree with Eric—communication *is* the most important thing that he does every day. Hoyle, English, and Steffy (1998) identify communication and community relations as one of the nine most important skills for leaders to master, while Arnold, Perry, Watson, Minatra, and Schwartz (2006) conclude that principals cannot be successful unless they communicate effectively with their publics. Marzano, Waters, and McNulty (2005) support findings from both of these studies, noting that the most accomplished principals establish strong lines of communication throughout the school community, and Strong, Richard, and Catano (2008) emphasize that principals who practice two-way communication engender support for their schools. To put it simply, communication should be the most important thing that *you* do every day.

While establishing strong lines of communication *within* the schoolhouse has always been essential for maintaining focus and for building momentum toward shared objectives, communication *beyond* the schoolhouse has become more important than ever. Faced with shrinking budgets and constant scrutiny in today's accountability culture, public relations has quickly become a new priority for principals. After all, informed communities tend to care more about their schools (Strong et al., 2008).

Public relations efforts allow principals to convincingly articulate a school's vision to stakeholders outside of the educational community. Public relations efforts also help school leaders to develop a brand presence, to keep key community members informed, and to build broad coalitions with businesses and community agencies, resulting in strong support for school programs and efforts. Principals who are successfully tapping into the goodwill of the communities that they serve are constantly listening, writing, speaking, and reading (McEwan, 2003), and are seen as accessible and responsive by their constituents.

In this chapter, we will explore the changing public relations patterns of effective principals. We will start by looking at the kinds of messages that build trust and goodwill within the community. Next, we will examine the limitations of the traditional communication strategies—mass mailings, electronic mailing lists, school websites, local newspapers—that have defined our efforts to reach beyond the walls of our buildings. Finally, we will explain how Twitter and Facebook, the most popular social media spaces, can be used to communicate with community members and to improve a building's brand presence.

Recognizing the Importance of School-Level Branding

Branding, a term synonymous with marketing and business, is beginning to find its niche in education. Brands promise value—essential for maintaining support in difficult economic conditions—to specific audiences or stakeholder groups. Brands are designed to stand out, to influence consumers, and to build confidence in products. Sustaining a sense of trust is an integral component of a brand's ability to promise value. Successful brands open themselves up to scrutiny, respond to criticism, make every effort to own up to their mistakes, and work to improve based on consumer feedback.

In education, schools are considered a brand, promising their communities the academic preparation necessary to succeed. Many families choose to live in townships with schools that have proven track records. Stakeholders become convinced that their schools prepare students well and provide a quality return on their investment of time, energy, and resources. Schools can leverage this brand presence for additional community investment in teacher quality, curriculum, facilities, and professional development initiatives. The bottom line is that schools actively building their brands are supported by their communities, and that support translates into continued improvement and success.

While there are many factors that go into building a school's brand, the following variables—standardized test scores, teacher and administrator quality, interesting instructional practices, and extracurricular activities—should make their way into your public relations efforts.

- **Standardized test scores:** Regardless of how educators feel about the validity of state and federal testing programs, well-intentioned outsiders use these scores to evaluate the overall effectiveness of schools. Finding evidence in annual exams—percentages of students in the highest performance categories, percentages of students showing growth from one year to the next, significant increases in the overall academic performance of your student population, and performance comparisons to similar student populations across the district and state—that can be acknowledged in public relations efforts sends the message that your building is measuring up against and making progress toward meeting external standards and expectations.

- **Teacher and administrator quality:** Any parent is likely to tell you that student achievement is directly linked to the quality of teachers in a building. That's why townships known for having large numbers of quality personnel are constantly growing and generally willing to pay higher taxes to attract and retain the best educators. Including statistics about the qualifications of your faculty in public relations efforts can build the confidence of your community.

- **Interesting instructional practices:** Interesting course offerings, curricular decisions, and instructional strategies are pivotal for keeping students engaged in school and have a significant impact on student outcomes (Whitehurst, 2009). More importantly, interesting offerings, curricula, and instructional strategies can make your school stand out compared to local rivals. Publicizing these offerings sends the message that your students have the flexibility to pursue their interests while preparing for middle school, high school, higher education, or employment.

- **Extracurricular activities:** Parents understand that extracurricular programs help to develop well-rounded students and to build self-esteem. Students who participate in after-school programs are more engaged in and have a healthier attitude about learning, enjoy a greater sense of accomplishment, and perform better academically (Miller, 2003). Using public relations efforts to spotlight your school's extracurricular programs will gain the attention of parents and community leaders alike.

The challenge here, however, is that public relations can get pushed aside in the flurry of tasks necessary for simply running the day-to-day operations of any building. What's more, even when principals decide to make public relations a priority, they quickly discover some common obstacles. First, the potential audience for typical school-branding efforts built around press releases in community newspapers or internally maintained websites is limited to community members who subscribe to those newspapers, have access to the Internet, or are committed to regularly tracking school communications.

Second, relying on external sources to communicate messages also means that schools must compete for the time and attention of local news media, which can result in important messages being overlooked completely. Maintaining control over messaging however—as when schools assume publishing responsibilities by printing and mailing regular newsletters to every family—can stretch already-limited budgets.

Complicating matters even more, schools are always competing for the attention of their communities. While maintaining control over publishing decisions ensures that important content is delivered, it does not guarantee that overwhelmed audiences—who tune out all but the most important information—will automatically consume messages that their schools create.

Finally, using traditional media for branding and communication does little to encourage give-and-take between schools and the communities they serve. While traditional media can deliver messages, receiving and responding to feedback is almost impossible. This lack of responsiveness can make schools seem aloof and uncaring. Worse yet, traditional means for branding and communication are inherently slow. By the time messages are crafted and delivered, they are also outdated and unimportant. This lag in message delivery runs contrary to the immediacy that defines communication in today's digital age.

The lesson to be learned is simple: while the content of our branding efforts hasn't changed in the past twenty years—standardized test scores, teacher and administrator quality, interesting instructional practices, and extracurricular activities have always been important indicators of successful schools—the consumption preferences of our audiences are changing. Fewer people are subscribing to newspapers, school websites are additional destinations that parents don't have the time to visit regularly, and email messages are lost in overflowing inboxes. Addressing these constraints depends on principals who are willing to utilize nontraditional tools and practices to communicate with stakeholders. As ZDNet Education writer Chris Dawson explains, "Businesses are meeting their potential customers on whatever channel makes their customers happy, whether that's a Facebook page, a website, emailed updates, text messages, or all of the above. Should parents and students actually expect any less of the schools for which their tax and/or tuition dollars pay?" (Dawson, 2011).

Or as Jennifer Cisney, Eastman Kodak's chief blogger and social media manager, explained in an interview with Amber Mac (2010), author of *Power Friending*, "Today, you can't expect everyone to come where you are. We have to go to them" (Kindle location 313–317).

Learning From the Business World

For Comcast, one of America's largest cable companies, *going to the people* began the day that an angry customer recorded a snoring technician sleeping on her couch and posted the video to YouTube (http://snipurl.com/snoringtechnician). With 1.4 million views, Comcast quickly became the laughingstock of the social media world (Israel, 2009).

Repairing this damaged reputation, interestingly enough, began with nothing more than a customer support employee named Frank Eliason and a Twitter account. Recognizing that people were using social media tools to share opinions on companies with their peers, Eliason began using Twitter to reach out to disgruntled customers under the username @ComcastCares. Armed with nothing more than the free tools and third-party applications described later in this chapter, Eliason began searching for references to Comcast in the messages that millions of Twitter users posted. What he found were frustrated customers venting about everything from weak signals to missed service calls (Israel, 2009).

While the criticism made him cringe, Eliason saw real opportunity in each negative message and started to reach out to customers. Like any of the millions of service representatives working in call centers around the world, he spent time troubleshooting common technical glitches and solving problems for over two thousand customers in the first year alone. The difference was that Eliason's work was done transparently and publicly online. Any of the thousands of people following Eliason's Twitter stream—@ComcastCares currently has just under 50,000 users watching its updates—saw a company interacting in a positive way with dissatisfied customers, instead of a company snoring on a leather couch. Comcast's reputation was literally repaired one Tweet at a time (Israel, 2009).

There are real lessons to be learned in Comcast's story for any school leader. Perhaps the most important lesson is that your stakeholders are talking about you whether you know it or not. Social media tools enable more people to connect with one another more often than ever before—and the messages that they are sharing are not always going to be positive.

Has the local paper just published standardized test results that appear on the surface to be less than flattering? Social media tools make it possible to quickly respond, pointing out individual areas of growth reporters overlook. Is a new private school opening in your district, enticing parents with beautiful facilities and state-of-the-art technology? With an active social media presence, you can remind constituents of your innovative schedule and highly qualified teaching staff. Regardless of your individual circumstances, managing your school's reputation depends on being aware of what your critics are saying.

Your stakeholders also need proof that you are listening. The businesses that have done the best job harnessing the power of social media tools to build their brands respond one message at a time. No concern is too trivial to address. Eliason explains, "We treat all our customers the same way. We don't care who they are. We care about fixing the problem" (as cited in Israel, 2009, Kindle location 887). By reaching out to everyone, Comcast has shown that they are willing to listen—and a willingness to listen generates goodwill.

Social media specialist Amber Mac (2010)—author of *Power Friending: Demystifying Social Media to Grow Your Business*—believes that developing positive relationships with important stakeholders in new digital spaces also requires authenticity, bravery, and consistency.

Authenticity

Our world has become an increasingly impersonal place in the past two decades. Instead of frequenting mom-and-pop shops down the street and talking to actual human beings when we need help with a product, we click our way around the Internet and spend hours poking through customer-service menus listening to prerecorded messages.

Sadly, parents and students often see schools as the same kinds of impersonal places. Once easily recognizable neighborhood icons, principals are often too busy to fully interact with their communities; high rates of transience in teacher and student populations make it unlikely that parents will have long-term relationships with faculty members; and standardized testing has created a culture that turns students into nothing more than numbers. The result of this impersonality is a general sense of distrust between individuals and the organizations that serve them.

Breaking through this distrust requires frequent, open interactions between stakeholders—behaviors that social media tools enable and amplify. Principals who take the time to respond honestly to teachers, students, parents, and community leaders in the digital forums they have already embraced will soon find that they are building communities of enthusiastic supporters who feel connected to one another and to their local schools for the first time.

Bravery

The greatest challenge for schools in a social media world is that the relationships between consumers and the businesses they support are changing. New tools have enabled progressive companies to interact directly and informally with customers in ways that were once impossible. They have also enabled businesses to craft interesting and exciting messages that entertain and capture attention.

As a result, education's stakeholders are beginning to expect the same kinds of innovative messaging from their schools. The static communication patterns that we have come to rely on are seen as standoffish and distant. Not only do these one-way messaging patterns fall short of the expectations of parents, students, younger staff members, and community leaders, they are likely to be lost in the digital noise that our communities are swimming in.

Being heard, then, requires bravery on the part of principals. We have to be willing to open ourselves to criticism and to interact directly with important stakeholders in order to be taken seriously. We also have to be willing to be inventive about the content and structure of the messages we are creating. While doing so is definitely risky in a field as staid as education, it carries tangible rewards in the form of stronger and more meaningful relationships with the communities we serve.

Consistency

Finally, incorporating social media tools into your school's communication patterns requires changing the way you see interactions with important stakeholders. Becoming active in social media circles means making a commitment to join conversations with teachers, parents, students, and community leaders—and joining conversations requires consistent participation. It is impossible to convince your stakeholders you are sincere about your desire to connect in social media spaces if you are rarely there!

That means new efforts to reach out using social media tools must be a priority. Carve out time in your day to visit the conversations developing between your stakeholders, whether they are happening on a blog, Facebook page, Twitter feed, or community bulletin board. Respond to questions. Post links to additional information. Gently correct misconceptions. Share pictures. Show that you are listening, because listening is a basic expectation that today's consumers hold for the organizations they follow online.

While consistently participating in social media spaces will require an additional investment of time and energy into your building's public relations efforts, the goodwill generated from two-way interactions in social media forums is exponential, spreading beyond just the individuals you are interacting with. That's because in a social media world, each resolution is played out in front of an audience. Every message has the potential to answer questions that others haven't asked. What's more, every message is a tangible demonstration—a minicommercial, so to speak—of your commitment to service. That tangible demonstration builds confidence in every customer, not just those having their problems solved (Israel, 2009).

For many principals, the open communication practices that Amber Mac advocates and Frank Eliason put into place at Comcast can be downright intimidating. We worry about parents and students using social media tools to complain about our decisions, our programs, or our performance. More importantly, we worry about those complaints being made in a public forum that anyone can view. Used to doing damage control anytime negative messages about our buildings surface, specifically creating forums that *enable* the easy sharing of negative messages runs contrary to our instincts.

Avoiding social media tools, however, is far riskier because they have been widely embraced beyond our buildings, fundamentally changing the nature of communication in today's world. Your important stakeholders—teachers, parents, students, and community leaders—"might not know it yet, and perhaps neither do you, but in just a few years if you haven't adopted social media in a significant way you risk shutting out the best and most powerful communications channel we've ever known, a channel that values authentic interactions . . . at its core" (Mac, 2010, Kindle location 76–81).

Using Twitter to Build Your School's Brand

The good news is that open-communication practices in a social media world don't have to be intimidating. For principals, experiments in open communication typically begin with Twitter (www.twitter.com) and Facebook (www.facebook.com). These two services have been broadly embraced across all social and technical profiles and make it possible to reach large audiences in the blink of an eye. More importantly, they enable the kinds of *two-way* interactions that made Comcast a social media success story—and a characteristic of the communication practices that consumers have grown to expect from businesses *and* schools (National School Boards Association, 2007).

Twitter and Facebook provide principals with real-time tools that are far superior to traditional forms of communication. Social media services paired with high rates of Internet connectivity allow multiple forms of information—web links, videos, audio files, images, text messages, and documents—to be delivered and consumed in multiple ways. With almost no effort, principals can share compelling, detailed messages that are readily accessible from mobile devices, tablets, and computers connected to the Internet with their school communities.

Implementing Twitter as a Communication Tool

The most approachable and least-intimidating tool for principals interested in using social media to connect with their communities is Twitter. One of the most popular microblogging platforms, Twitter allows users to post short, 140-character text-based messages called *tweets* to a designated page on the Internet. Tweets often point viewers to other web-based resources, providing principals with the means to deliver real-time school information in a matter of seconds.

Since each tweet is limited to 140 characters—the average length of one well-written sentence—messages are easy to generate for busy administrators. More importantly, updates to a school's Twitter website—commonly called a *Twitter stream*—can be made from *any* device that has access to the Internet, enabling on-the-go communication. (See figure 1.1 for a visual.) Principals using Twitter can always craft messages from traditional locations like their offices, but with cell phones, PDAs, or Internet-connected mobile devices, they can also begin messaging from the sidelines of the homecoming game, the back row of the band's first concert, or the table with the winning entry in the school's science fair.

Imagine using Twitter to immediately communicate the following to stakeholders.

- **Calendar reminders:** The school year is full of important dates. Twitter can be used to remind parents and students of athletic and performance schedules, standardized testing dates, end of marking periods, upcoming holidays, and school closings.

- **Celebrations:** The school year is also full of accomplishments. Sadly, publicly celebrating the successes of students and teachers can be hard to do in a timely fashion. Twitter allows immediate announcements of great achievements to the entire community.

- **Helpful resources:** Most parents would be happy to extend learning beyond the school day if they had the knowledge and skills needed to support their children. With Twitter, it's easy to share links to valuable web-based resources on parenting, teaching, or the content being studied in your classrooms.

Figure 1.1: Sample Twitter stream.

- **Decisions and details:** Schools and the organizations that support them are constantly making decisions with far-reaching implications. Boards of education pass new grading or promotion standards, parent-teacher organizations sponsor after-school programs or grade-level field trips, and booster clubs and educational foundations fund scholarships for struggling students. Using Twitter to share these decisions spreads information quickly and makes the inner workings of your organization transparent to everyone.

- **Emergency updates:** While principals never want to imagine scenarios for dealing with school-based emergencies, planning communication patterns before natural disasters or human tragedies strike is a responsible practice. Because Twitter updates can be posted from mobile devices, they can become a part of a comprehensive plan for easing community fears and getting messages out to parents and support professionals in emergency situations.

Getting Started With Twitter

For coauthor Eric Sheninger, using Twitter began by taking about five minutes to create a free account that communicated a bit of general information about his school. Knowing that he first needed a username that would be easy for parents and students to remember, he chose *NewMilfordHS.* The NewMilfordHS Twitter account follows a clear naming structure that parents could probably guess even if they weren't sure of the school's Twitter name. The direct address for New Milford's Twitter stream, www.twitter.com/newmilfordhs, is posted on the school's website and shared in as many parent messages as possible.

The second step to making any school-based Twitter stream easy to find is filling out the simple bio information that Twitter publicly displays about each user. Eric included a short sentence explaining that NewMilfordHS is a Twitter stream for New Milford High School in Bergen County, New Jersey, so that the parents and students could be certain that they had landed in the right place when checking Twitter for updates. To make the page stand out and to establish a brand presence, he used the school's colors, mascot, and logo; he also provided a direct link to the school's website.

Once a school's Twitter account has been created, updates can be added at any time. In fact, Eric started posting messages immediately, trying to see just what he had gotten himself into. Within minutes, he shared details about an upcoming parent night, a celebration of students on his school's honor roll, and a link on parenting teenagers he thought his community might find interesting. He explains, "To get that information on our traditional website would have taken a week's worth of emails and action by two or three different staff members" (Sheninger, 2010c).

Principals using Twitter to reach out to the communities they serve, however, may discover that initial efforts to use Twitter as a tool for school-based communication are met with raised eyebrows. While most of the adults in any community are likely to have heard of Twitter—recent studies estimate that 87 percent of Americans are aware of the service—only 7 percent of Americans actively use it (Webster, 2010). Parents and other important stakeholders may see such efforts as fads until they are shown what communication in social media spaces looks like in action. Without convincing your community that your school's Twitter stream is a valuable source of information, your work in Twitter will quickly become obsolete.

For Eric, that convincing began by crafting a written description of how Twitter would be used in his building. (See "Introducing Stakeholders to Twitter," page 24.) This description, which is shared with parents several times each year, provides a brief description of how Twitter differs from other social-networking tools. Next, his description explains the three different ways that parents can follow updates posted on Twitter: by signing up for their own Twitter account, by receiving updates as text messages, or by bookmarking New Milford's Twitter page for future reference. While the majority of New Milford High School's parents and students just visit the school's Twitter stream on the web to view updates, several are signed up to receive text messages when new content is posted, and well over one hundred follow New Milford's posts with their own Twitter accounts. Eric explains, "That versatility—allowing parents to receive updates on their own terms—makes Twitter unlike any traditional communication tool that I've ever used as a principal" (Sheninger, 2010a).

Options for posting updates to a school's Twitter stream are just as versatile. While the most common strategy for adding messages is signing in to the Twitter website, principals who grow comfortable with Twitter are inevitably drawn to third-party applications that increase Twitter's functionality. Free to download and easy to install on any computer, these applications allow users to search Twitter for posts about particular topics, create specialized groups of Twitter users worth following, and easily share other users' messages—a practice known as *retweeting*. TweetDeck, HootSuite, and Seesmic are third-party applications that are highly polished and popular.

TweetDeck

Available for PCs or Macs, TweetDeck (www.tweetdeck.com) allows users to break their Twitter feeds into customizable categories. Interested in following the Twitter streams of other schools to see how they use Twitter? Want to compile a collection of links to interesting articles posted by educational publications? Know of other principals whose Twitter updates you want to see in one place? TweetDeck columns make that possible. (See figure 1.2.)

Figure 1.2: Sample Twitter stream using TweetDeck.

TweetDeck also includes useful tools that allow users to post pictures, manage multiple accounts, translate messages into different languages, conduct searches, and shorten long web addresses and tweets—an essential feature for Twitter users, considering the 140-character length limit for individual messages. Finally, users can connect with their contacts across a variety of social networks including Facebook, LinkedIn, and foursquare, making TweetDeck a one-stop shop for principals interested in using social media for personal and professional communication.

HootSuite

HootSuite (http://hootsuite.com) is a web-based Twitter application that does not need to be downloaded—an important consideration for educators in districts with tight controls over content installed on computers. New users just have to visit the site and sign up. Like TweetDeck, HootSuite provides a social media dashboard where users can create columns and post updates to a wide range of social networks like Facebook, Flickr, and LinkedIn in one place and at one time.

HootSuite also allows users to create tweets in advance and release them according to a pre-determined schedule, to automatically shorten web addresses in new messages, to allow multiple editors to make posts from the same account, and to track interesting statistics (like total clicks, daily clicks, clicks by region, or popularity as compared to other messages) associated with each tweet. Finally, HootSuite users can install an add-on called *the Hootlet* in their Internet browser bar that makes sharing web pages in Twitter instant and easy.

Seesmic

Available for PC or Mac users, Seesmic (www.seesmic.com) is available in web, desktop, and mobile forms. The web-based option requires no downloads or installation and allows users to access their Twitter accounts from any Internet-connected device. Like both TweetDeck and HootSuite, Seesmic also allows users to organize tweets into columns. Useful Seesmic tools include full integration with Facebook, tweet translation services for multiple languages, and a profile page.

Tweeting From Your Phone

For many principals, posting updates to Twitter streams from mobile devices adds a new degree of flexibility to school-based communication patterns. With more and more districts issuing smartphones to their principals to enable remote access to email, the Internet, and district calendar programs, mobile posting to Twitter is an approachable and logical next step worth exploring. Frequent real-time updates shared from important events—like championship athletic contests, essential school board meetings, and school-based academic competitions or performances—can allow parents and community members to follow developments easily from any Internet-enabled device.

What's more, principals who take advantage of the cameras in their smartphones can add interactive content to any Twitter stream. Pictures and videos can be immediately uploaded to Twitter. Imagine the interest and goodwill that can be generated by instantly sharing pictures of student projects entered in the school's art show, recordings from the school's musical performances, or video from the school's mock-trial competition—all practices made possible with nothing more than smartphones and Twitter accounts.

Like the third-party applications that users can download to their computers, there are literally dozens of free programs that can make working with Twitter on mobile devices easy. While these programs are generally stripped-down versions of their full-featured cousins, they all enable users to post quick text-, picture-, and video-based messages to their Twitter streams. For principals who rarely wander far from their smartphones, this functionality is both exciting and essential. If you are interested in tweeting from your mobile phone, consider exploring one of the following applications: Twitter Mobile, TweetDeck for iPhone, or Seesmic Mobile.

Twitter Mobile

Twitter has developed its own application for BlackBerry, Android, and iPhone devices. It varies slightly depending on the device it is running on, but can be downloaded via each brand's respective app store. Perhaps the most unique feature of the official Twitter application—outside its deep integration with each respective operating system—is the ability for users to link to their Twitter contacts, a functionality that other mobile applications often leave out.

TweetDeck for iPhone

Similar to the desktop application highlighted earlier in this chapter, the TweetDeck mobile app (www.tweetdeck.com/iphone) allows iPhone users to organize their Twitter stream in columns on an iPhone, iPad, or iPod touch. Other useful features include geolocation (the ability to find, and to be found by, other Twitter users in your general area), Facebook integration, multiple-account management (the ability to message from an individual account and a school-based account using one login), photo and video sharing, and automatic link shortening. Users can easily refresh their Twitter streams in the TweetDeck mobile app by shaking their phones.

Seesmic Mobile

Also similar to the desktop application highlighted earlier in this chapter, Seesmic Mobile (http://seesmic.com/seesmic_mobile) operates on various mobile platforms, but is the app of choice on Android-based phones. It allows users to access multiple accounts, contains a unique widget—a small application that can be installed and implemented from the website—so a single tweet will never be missed in the timeline, and supports the sharing of videos, photos, and locations.

For many Twitter users, choosing a mobile application is a personal decision made only after experimenting with several different options. For some, having the increased functionality that services like the Twitter app, TweetDeck for iPhone, and Seesmic Mobile offer maximizes the utility of their mobile devices. For others, extra functions become additional distractions and require a bigger learning curve. Remaining flexible and open to change is the best strategy for finding a mobile application that works for you.

Twittering Fosters Professional Partnerships

While the primary purpose of every school-based Twitter stream should be to communicate with parents and to build broad coalitions with community advocates, principals who begin tweeting will inevitably make valuable connections and build professional relationships with other educators and companies—like professional developers, technology service providers, researchers, and notable education magazines and publishers—charged with supporting schools. Cultivating these connections can lead to ongoing partnerships that hold value for schools and districts.

One of the most powerful partnerships New Milford High has forged through Twitter communications has been with AVerMedia, a company that supplies schools with innovative educational technology tools. After connecting with an AVerMedia representative through a referral from another educator on Twitter, Eric's school was selected as an AVerAcademy, seeded with the company's latest technologies, and provided with ongoing professional development for faculty members.

New Milford ended up receiving two free, state-of-the-art document cameras and two sets of digital pens that can be used as student responders. Company representatives also visited the school twice in 2009–2010, providing hands-on training on the effective classroom integration of these new technologies. In return, teachers from New Milford High share lesson ideas and success stories with AVerMedia—and have their efforts highlighted in the continuing work that the company does with teachers worldwide.

Principals who embrace Twitter for school-based communications are likely to fall in love with it quickly. In its simplest form, it is a tool that makes posting short updates on school happenings easy for everyone. No longer are there long delays between the crafting and sharing of important messages. It is also one of the most versatile social media tools available, allowing users to message from a wide range of devices and applications. Finally, it is a tool that enables principals to cultivate powerful partnerships with professionals beyond the local community. Eric notes, "I'm not sure how I ever lived without it. While becoming a major part of our school's communication plan, Twitter has also become a major part of my own professional learning patterns" (Sheninger, 2010d).

Implementing Facebook as a Communication Tool

With over 500 million registered users, Facebook has established itself as the social media site of choice for almost anyone interested in using digital tools to keep in touch with friends and family ("Statistics," n.d.). Like Twitter, principals can take advantage of this immense social network to engage students, parents, and interested community members. Unlike Twitter, these audiences are much more likely to be knowledgeable and comfortable with Facebook because it has been in the mainstream for a longer period of time.

The challenge, however, is that Facebook has garnered its fair share of negative press in school circles. There have been frequent stories about students using the site for cyberbullying, continuing fears of chance interactions between teens and Internet predators, and repeated incidents of poor choices made by educators who forget that their responsibility as role models doesn't end when they are living online. This has caused some districts to specifically ban employees from interacting with parents and students on Facebook.

So why even consider using Facebook—a tool that school and districts often scorn—as a part of your communications plan? Perhaps most importantly, Facebook *is* an important part of the lives of today's students—a group that schools often overlook in their efforts to build partnerships.

For tweens and teens, Facebook is a digital home. Frequently logging in several times each day, middle and high school students use Facebook to keep in touch with friends. They are making plans and forming groups on Facebook (Lenhart & Madden, 2007). They are sending messages and sharing photos. They are giving and receiving advice (Hampton, Sessions, Her, & Rainie, 2009). In *Hanging Out, Messing Around, and Geeking Out,* danah boyd (2010) explains, "By providing tools for mediated interactions, social media allow teens to extend their interactions beyond physical boundaries. Conversations and interactions that begin in person do not end when friends are separated" (p. 80).

Facebook, then, gives school leaders working in middle and high schools the means to extend their interactions with students beyond the physical boundaries of their buildings. Traditional messages—like schedule changes, results of athletic contests, and important reminders of upcoming events—are more likely to reach students when posted on Facebook than when shared in any other forum, simply because Facebook is the primary communication tool for digitally connected tweens and teens. Innovative principals can even use Facebook to provide students with opportunities to give feedback on school policies and practices—a step toward transparency that teens value and appreciate.

Using Facebook isn't just about reaching your students, though. In fact, Facebook is also the most important web destination for many adults, who already see the service as a tool for keeping up with organizations. The average Facebook user is connected to eighty different community groups or events ("Statistics," n.d.). Principals who embrace Facebook, then, cater to the communication patterns of their communities, designing messages that are more likely to be seen because they are delivered in a forum that their stakeholders have embraced.

Finally, Facebook facilitates communication *among* stakeholder groups—a practice that traditional communication tools rarely enable. Parents can learn about the value of individual school programs from alumni who visit a school's page to share what they know. Teachers can tailor their instructional practices after listening to students who write about memorable lessons and activities. Business leaders can quickly identify the most pressing needs of a school after interacting with parents and teachers who have firsthand awareness of current realities. Principals act as catalysts for these cross-group interactions by initiating conversations specific to their school.

Getting Started With Facebook

Getting started with Facebook at the school level begins by understanding the anatomy of a *Facebook page*—the common term describing a user's site. Each Facebook is actually a collection of several individual page links that are sorted by sections that are listed under the user's profile picture and include their own customizable settings. While users can add as many pages to a Facebook as they like, the wall, information, photos and videos, events, and a discussion board are the most common for schools using Facebook to reach out to families.

The Wall

An interactive space that allows users to post short messages known as status updates from any Internet-connected device, the wall is the core element of any Facebook. As with Twitter, principals using Facebook can share everything from schedule changes and updates about school events to interesting articles and valuable resources on their school's wall. Along with appearing automatically on the news feed of the Facebook pages of users who have chosen to follow a school's updates, these short messages are also instantly visible to anyone who visits a school's Facebook page on the web.

Information

Adding an information page to a school's Facebook allows principals to collect and organize important contact details in one location. By listing a school's address, hours of operation, parking locations, telephone number, and website links on an information page, principals can answer many of the most common questions before they are even asked.

Photos and Videos

In an increasingly digital world, photos and videos are important tools for both persuasion and communication. Almost 85 percent of all Americans report watching videos on the Internet—logging 31 billion views every month—and 50 percent are sharing pictures online (Lipsman, 2010; n.a., 2009). Capturing the attention of audiences, then, depends on building interactive school websites that incorporate visual messages. The photos and videos pages of a Facebook can provide a digital home for this kind of engaging content.

Events

Acting like common online calendar applications, the events link on a Facebook page allows principals to keep everyone abreast of important dates and times. Users adding events to a Facebook are asked several simple questions designed to share important details with viewers—When?, What are you planning?, Where?, More info?, and Who's invited? Once created, individual events can be posted as status updates on a school's Facebook wall or shared with specific Facebook users.

Discussion Board

Perhaps the most underutilized page that principals can add to their school's Facebook is a discussion board. While it can be intimidating to encourage stakeholders to engage in ongoing conversations with one another, discussions also provide school leaders with a great deal of flexibility. Principals can elicit feedback from specific groups—including students—on initiatives, programs, or events, gathering insights that may have otherwise gone overlooked. Alumni groups can also use discussion boards to coordinate reunions.

Notice that both Twitter and Facebook allow users to post short messages to the web from any Internet-connected device. Facebook is far more sophisticated, however, allowing users to manage growing collections of pictures, videos, and conversations. While Facebook sites require more work to maintain and to monitor, they can—over time—complement a school's static website by providing an interactive, networked home for parents, students, and alumni.

Once you have decided that you'd like to use Facebook to reach out to your school community, you will need to create a personal Facebook account. Not only will experimenting as an individual help you to better understand the professional uses of Facebook, a registered account is required in order to access the page-building tools and features necessary for developing a unique Facebook for your organization. Creating your own Facebook account will also enable you to be the administrator of your school's new page, guaranteeing that you can control all of the content that appears on your site. It should be noted, though, that even though a personal Facebook account is required to create a Facebook for your school, none of your personal information will be visible on your school's page. Developing a Facebook for your school then begins by selecting the *Create a Page* tool (www.facebook.com/pages/create.php).

After answering a few general questions about the organization that you represent and categorizing the Facebook that you are trying to create, you will have the chance to personalize your school's page—a process that should include uploading a photo of your school or mascot to establish a brand presence for your new Facebook. Doing so can ensure that visitors to your page will quickly be able to identify your site as an official tool for disseminating important school information.

After uploading a photo, Facebook will ask you to provide additional information that describes your page. Consider using this space to share links to official school or district websites, to your building's Twitter stream, or to other school groups that have created a presence on Facebook—such as athletic teams, alumni groups, or after-school organizations—in order to build connections and to increase the communicative power of your Facebook.

Finally, you will be asked to choose the kinds of sections—photo and video collections, discussion boards, and information pages—that you'd like to include on your site. Consider starting with a wall for posting quick school-based status updates and an events section for sharing your school's calendar. As you grow more comfortable with your developing community, you can easily add additional features and pages.

Once you have created your school's Facebook, the last step is to begin advertising. Share links on your traditional website and in mass mailings. Include links in your email's auto signature. Ask your teachers to include links in their messages to parents and students. Spotlight your new site at parent nights, business roundtable discussions, and community gatherings. You are likely to find that your Facebook will gain followers and attention quickly. In fact, as long as you continue to add content, your Facebook page will probably see more monthly visitors than your traditional website in no time. Eric explains, "There are so many people already using Facebook to interact with their friends and family. They're always excited to find out that they can learn about our school at the same time" (Sheninger, 2010e).

Next Steps

For over a decade, educational researchers have been sharing one consistent message: effective principals seek out opportunities on a regular basis to actively engage the communities they serve (Beck & Murphy, 1996). The challenge for today's principals, however, is that society's definition of *active engagement* changes as rapidly as the tools we use to communicate. No longer are occasional newsletters sent home on school letterhead or are occasional updates to static websites enough to satisfy stakeholders. Instead, engagement begins with the kinds of social media tools that individuals and corporations beyond the schoolhouse walls have embraced.

And while incorporating social media tools like Twitter and Facebook into your communication plan can be initially intimidating, it is not an impossible process. To turn the challenge of communicating in a digital age into an opportunity, reflect on your current communication patterns, experiment with social media tools, explore how other schools are using social media tools, start small, and communicate your changing practices to stakeholders.

Reflect on Your Current Communication Patterns

Redesigning your school's communication plan begins by gathering as much feedback as you can about your current efforts to share messages with stakeholders. This knowledge—which can be gathered easily by using the "21st Century Communications Rubric" (page 25) and the "School Communication Survey" (page 27)—will help you to better understand the kinds of changes that will resonate with your community.

Experiment With Social Media Tools

While they are not often publicly stated, there are clear norms for participation in most social media spaces that include language structures for crafting posts, expectations for following other users, and strong beliefs about the kinds of messages that should and should not be shared. Learning about these norms—and thinking through how they are likely to influence your efforts to redesign your school's communication plan—can best be accomplished by experimenting with social media tools as an individual first.

Sign up for Twitter and Facebook, and then, for a while, quietly *lurk*—the digital description for members of social networks who are listening without posting. Watch the interactions that occur between people. Notice the content of messages that are well received. Figure out how digital connections develop. Study the process of network building and collective sharing. Doing so will help you understand the features of the social media tool that you are considering for your communication plan, and will help you identify regular examples of the rewards that can come from instant sharing in the digital forums that have been embraced beyond our schools.

Explore How Other Schools Are Using Social Media Tools

As you experiment with social media tools, you will inevitably begin wondering just how other schools are using the same tools to interact with their stakeholders. When you are ready to answer this question, consider exploring the work of several of the elementary, middle, and high schools included in the "Exploring School-Based Social Media Efforts" handout (page 29).

Identify the different kinds of content they are sharing. Notice any new risks they are taking. Check out how many "followers" or "friends" they have gathered. Make note of the practices you could integrate into your own work quickly—as well as the practices you would stay away from. Seeing school efforts with social media might just help you to solidify your decision to incorporate Twitter streams and Facebook pages into your own communication plan.

Start Small

The biggest barrier to successfully integrating social media tools into your school's communication plan is often your own level of energy and enthusiasm. New practices can be initially frustrating—and they will stay that way until you have established a comfortable routine for interacting with the new content and opportunities you are creating. As a result, starting small is a must. By sticking with simple goals and patterns—like posting twice a day, sharing links instead of creating videos, and reviewing and responding to messages once a week—you will prevent the inevitable exhaustion that comes with radical changes.

For many principals new to social media spaces, *starting small* also means starting with Twitter primarily because maintaining a professional presence in Facebook requires more monitoring and management than maintaining a professional presence in Twitter. Visitors to a school's Facebook page expect to see pictures and videos of teachers. They expect to see ongoing moderated conversations about school happenings. They expect to see advertisements for upcoming events and links to contact information.

Visitors to a school's Twitter stream expect to see nothing more than quick announcements, short thoughts, and the occasional link to external resources. That means Twitter requires less time and energy from principals who are just beginning to experiment with social media spaces. While it may be a tool that parents know less about, it is also a tool that principals can manage and maintain easier.

Remember that no matter how small your efforts are, however, you will need parent permission before using student names and likenesses in any school-based communications. While posting photos, videos, or text-based messages celebrating the successes of individual students can build goodwill in the community and add a more human touch to your school's social media efforts, failing to respect the privacy wishes of your parents is a mistake that is impossible to repair. If your district hasn't already developed a release form asking for permission to use student names and likenesses, consider using the "New Media Parent Release" (page 31) as a guide for developing your own. Familiarize yourself with the stakeholders in your district's central office—members of the school's senior leadership, employees in charge of district communication efforts, lawyers that represent the school or district—that will want to have a voice in the development of your new media parent release form. How will you reach out to those stakeholders before sharing any form with the parents of your school community? Consider the strengths and weaknesses of this new media parent release form, the questions stakeholders will have after reading it, and how you would incorporate answers to similar questions in your own letter.

Communicate Your Changing Practices to Stakeholders

It is also important to remember that using social media tools to communicate with stakeholders is likely to be a new practice for your parents and students as well. While most will have heard of—and many will already be using—Twitter and Facebook, it is unlikely that they will have experience interacting with schools in these forums. That means building awareness of your efforts in your local community is essential for ensuring that your new communication plan is a success.

To build awareness, consider crafting and sharing introductory letters outlining your intentions for social media tools and explaining how your new messages can be found online. The handout titled "Introducing Stakeholders to Twitter"—mentioned earlier in this chapter and found on page 24—might serve as a starting point for your awareness efforts.

At some point, though, stop reflecting and take action! Through trial and error, you will quickly identify social media practices that you are comfortable with and create new plans for reaching your stakeholders in the forums they are already drawn to.

Introducing Stakeholders to Twitter

Yes, Even New Milford High School Is Tweeting!

By now, you've probably heard of the popular social-networking service Twitter (www.twitter.com), right? After all, every celebrity from Oprah to Ellen—and every business from Southwest Airlines to Denny's—seems to have an account!

I'd love for you to give Twitter a chance, too, because I'm planning on using it to increase communication with the New Milford High School community! You see, Twitter makes it easy for me to *instantaneously* disseminate useful information— testing dates, progress report schedules, scores from athletic events, emergency closings, links to valuable online resources for parents and students, and more. I can even post photos and videos of NMHS happenings from my cell phone, allowing us to celebrate the successes of our teachers and our students more frequently than ever before.

The best part is the messages shared in our school's Twitter stream are short and available to you in a bunch of different ways. For most parents and students, visiting our school's Twitter page (www.twitter.com/NewMilfordHS) will probably be the best option.

If you're already using Twitter to communicate with friends, family, or colleagues— or if you're willing to create a free Twitter account to experiment with—you can follow our updates automatically by searching for @NewMilfordHS from your Twitter homepage. You can even have our messages delivered automatically to your cell phone as text messages!

And if you're up for an adventure, you can follow the messages that I share in my professional Twitter account (www.twitter.com/NMHS_Principal), but be forewarned that I tweet excessively about education and partake in chats with educators from all over the world on ways to increase student achievement!

I'm really proud of what we're doing here at New Milford High School. Our teachers and students are some of the best in the state, and I'm thankful for the support of our community. Twitter makes it possible for me to easily share our successes and to keep you up to date on what we're doing. We're excited about this communication tool and already using it on a regular basis—so I hope you'll consider giving us a look.

Regards,

Eric Sheninger

Principal, New Milford High School

21st Century Communications Rubric

Researchers have shown time and again that highly effective principals are highly effective communicators, engaging their communities in ongoing conversations about teaching and learning. The challenge for today's principal is that while the nature of our messages haven't changed—parents still need to understand a school's vision, community leaders still need to know how to best support our schools, and students still need to find connections between what they're learning in school today and what they'll need to be successful tomorrow—yesterday's communication tools are ineffective. Consider using this rubric to evaluate the currency of your school's communication plan.

Scoring Your School's Communication Plans

LEVEL 3

Messages can be delivered and received anytime and from any place using an Internet-connected device. Messages regularly include interactive content—like video clips from school performances, photos from athletic events, podcast recordings of important messages, and links to external sites for continued exploration—captured and shared in real time. While customized for individual stakeholder groups and often shared in traditional ways, messages can also be accessible to broader audiences and posted in several different social media forums in an effort to reach out to digitally connected parents, students, and stakeholders. Messages are crafted and delivered instantly at the school level. The principal has complete control and flexibility over message frequency and content. Messaging patterns provide ongoing opportunities for two-way interaction between stakeholders and school staff members. The principal transparently demonstrates a willingness to listen and to respond to the community.

Overall, this communication plan shows extensive evidence that the school is listening to—and interacting with—the communities it serves. School leaders have clearly worked to establish footprints in popular social media services and are regularly initiating conversations with all important audiences. What's more, they are crafting engaging messages likely to catch the attention of today's parents, students, and stakeholders. Finally, this communication plan is defined by its versatility, allowing audiences to interact with school messages in a variety of different forums and with a variety of different devices.

LEVEL 2

Messages are shared in several different formats. Static websites, newsletters, phone messages, community newspapers, press releases, and electronic mailing lists are all used in an attempt to reach wider audiences. The school's website shows clear efforts to craft engaging messages and to capture the attention of today's audiences. Video messages are embedded, audio content is posted, and collections of links are updated and maintained. While there is no evidence of real-time communication or complete flexibility on the part of the principal to reach out to important audiences, messages are current, reflecting a genuine commitment to sharing school happenings. The principal regularly responds to interested stakeholders, but those interactions happen in one-to-one situations that the school rarely initiates.

Overall, this communication plan shows willingness on the part of the school to share interesting and timely messages with the communities it serves. Content created is engaging and likely to stand out to today's parents, students, and stakeholders. There is little evidence, however, that the school is willing to listen to or interact with audiences. Communication patterns are largely one-dimensional—staff members deliver while constituents passively receive. Little has been done to establish footprints in popular social media services.

LEVEL 1

Messages are generally delivered in limited formats—a weekly newsletter sent home with students, a Monday's Message from the principal, or an occasional article in the community newspaper. The school relies heavily on a static, text-heavy website to reach online audiences. Sharing messages is a time-consuming, multistep process that depends on the action of several different employees. Messages shared are often out of date, lending a sense of apathy to the school's communication efforts. There are no opportunities for message recipients to respond to or interact with one another. There are no opportunities for message recipients to respond to or interact with school employees.

Overall, this communication plan shows little evidence that the school is listening to—and interacting with—the communities it serves. There seem to be no efforts to reach out to constituents by using popular social media services. What's more, there seem to be no efforts to provide opportunities for constituents to interact with messages that the school shares. Finally, there seem to be no efforts to craft the kinds of interactive, engaging messages that today's parents, students, and stakeholders have grown to expect.

School Communication Survey

This survey is designed to collect information from parents, students, and other interested stakeholders about our school's communication patterns.

Please circle your role in our community :   Parent   Student   Other stakeholder

Background Information

Please circle the number that best describes your own communication patterns.

	Never	Sometimes	Always
1. I read the local community newspaper.	1	2	3
2. I watch community programming on local access television.	1	2	3
3. I use texting, instant messaging, or both to communicate with family, friends, and colleagues.	1	2	3
4. When they're available, I watch digital videos posted online.	1	2	3
5. I access the Internet from a mobile device—such as a cell phone, iPad, iPod touch, or gaming device.	1	2	3
6. I spend time networking with friends and family on Facebook.	1	2	3
7. I spend time interacting with businesses and community groups on Facebook.	1	2	3
8. I spend time networking with friends and family on Twitter.	1	2	3
9. I spend time following the updates of business and community groups on Twitter.	1	2	3
10. I struggle to keep up with the important messages in my life.	1	2	3

School Communication Questions

Please circle the number that indicates the extent to which you agree or disagree with the following statements concerning our school's communication patterns. Then, indicate how important each expectation is to you.

Message Delivery and Engagement	Disagree	Neutral	Agree	Not Important	Somewhat Important	Very Important
1. Our school communicates important information—openings, closings, and schedules—in a timely and effective manner.	1	2	3	1	2	3
2. Our school regularly communicates student successes including academic achievements, athletic results, and visual/performing arts accomplishments.	1	2	3	1	2	3
3. Our school markets itself well by publicly sharing interesting course offerings and after-school clubs.	1	2	3	1	2	3
4. Our school regularly shares news about the qualifications and accomplishments of its teachers.	1	2	3	1	2	3

Message Delivery and Engagement	Disagree	Neutral	Agree	Not Important	Somewhat Important	Very Important
5. I can receive messages from our school in a variety of different ways—through my cell phone or mobile device, in print, or from my computer.	1	2	3	1	2	3
6. Our school's website is an engaging destination that I always look forward to exploring.	1	2	3	1	2	3
7. I would like to see more photos and videos of school happenings shared on our school's website.	1	2	3	1	2	3
8. I am satisfied with the way I'm currently receiving messages from our school.	1	2	3	1	2	3
9. The messages our school shares regularly catch my attention and stand out from the messages shared by the other organizations—businesses, community groups, and workplaces—in my life.	1	2	3	1	2	3
10. Our school's messages leave me confident and proud to live in this community.	1	2	3	1	2	3

Transparency and Interaction	Disagree	Neutral	Agree	Not Important	Somewhat Important	Very Important
1. I expect the organizations in my life—businesses, schools, and religious and community groups—to publicly interact with their members.	1	2	3	1	2	3
2. I value organizations—businesses, schools, and religious and community groups—that are responsive, publicly collecting feedback and openly responding to concerns.	1	2	3	1	2	3
3. I am aware of the efforts that our school makes to collect and to act on feedback from our community.	1	2	3	1	2	3
4. I am satisfied with the efforts that our school makes to collect and to act on feedback from our community.	1	2	3	1	2	3
5. Our school respects and values dissenting opinions.	1	2	3	1	2	3
6. Our school is open and honest in its dealings with stakeholders.	1	2	3	1	2	3
7. I would interact with our school more often if it used social media services like Facebook and Twitter.	1	2	3	1	2	3

Exploring School-Based Social Media Efforts

One of the best ways to build confidence in your own social media communication plan is to explore the efforts of other schools. This handout can help you to track your reactions while exploring the social media efforts of some selected schools and principals. You may find and track others as well.

School	Social Media Tool	Web Address
Conrad Ball Middle School Loveland, Colorado Scott Elias, principal	Twitter	http://twitter.com/scottelias
Hamilton Elementary School Chicago, Illinois James Gray, principal	Twitter	http://twitter.com/HamiltonCPS
John F. Kennedy Middle School Atlanta, Georgia Lucious Brown, principal	Twitter	http://twitter.com/johnfkennedyms
Lady's Island Middle School Beaufort, South Carolina Martin Wright, principal	Facebook	http://bit.ly/limiddle
New Milford High School New Milford, New Jersey Eric Sheninger, principal	Twitter Twitter Facebook	http://twitter.com/newmilfordhs http://twitter.com/NMHS_Principal http://bit.ly/newmilfordhs
Peace River Elementary School Port Charlotte, Florida Bertie Alvarez, principal	Facebook	http://bit.ly/peaceriveres
Willard East Elementary Willard, Missouri Melinda Miller, principal	Twitter	http://twitter.com/mmiller7571

Communicating and Connecting With Social Media © 2011 Solution Tree Press • solution-tree.com
Visit **go.solution-tree.com/technology** to download this page.

Name and location of school:		
Messaging Content	**Messaging Engagement**	**Responsiveness**
What types of messages is this school sharing in social media? *(Check all that apply.)* ☐ Calendar reminders ☐ Celebrations ☐ Helpful resources ☐ Decisions and details ☐ Emergency updates Which messages seem to be shared most often? Which do you think stakeholders find the most valuable?	How is this school crafting messages that will catch the attention of its audiences? *(Check all that apply.)* ☐ Sharing links to photos ☐ Sharing links to videos ☐ Sharing links to valuable resources ☐ Posting content in real time ☐ Providing opportunities for audiences to interact and respond to school messages Is the content this school is sharing more or less engaging than the content you're currently sharing with your stakeholders? Why? Why not?	What evidence of two-way communication can you find in this school's social media efforts? *(Check all that apply.)* ☐ School explicitly asks for input from stakeholders on important topics. ☐ Stakeholders have the ability to respond to every message. ☐ School responds to every message that a stakeholder posts. ☐ Dissenting opinions are respected in two-way interactions between school and stakeholders. ☐ Stakeholders are comfortable enough to respond to one another's questions and concerns in social media forums.

Reflections

What was impressive about the communication patterns of this school? What would you replicate in your own school?

Was there anything in the communication patterns of this school that left you concerned? Intimidated? Why?

What kinds of practical action steps would you have to take if you wanted to start similar communication patterns in your own school? Would new tools be needed? New training? New permissions?

New Media Parent Release

Dear Parents,

One of the things that we take great pride in at our school is our efforts to share important information with our stakeholders in a variety of ways. Not only will we use traditional tools—newsletters, phone calls, local papers, and websites—to keep you posted about everything happening here in our building, we'll also use social media services like Twitter and Facebook. We hope to develop stronger partnerships with the community we serve by joining you in these popular digital spaces.

We also like to celebrate the successes of our students in all of our communications. There are times when we'll share photos or video clips from important school events like dances, performances, athletic events, or interesting classroom activities. We also like to praise students who are doing remarkable things in and beyond our classrooms. We believe that we build stronger communities when we take the time to spotlight the positive work our children do.

Understandably, however, we want to respect your right to privacy. As a result, we'd like to know which of the following practices you give us permission to use in our school-based communication efforts:

(Please check all that apply.)

☐ **I give permission for my child's first and last name** to be used in any school-based communications—like newsletters, websites, articles for local papers, television programs, and posts to school-monitored social media spaces—that school or district employees generate.

☐ **I give permission for my child's likeness** to be used in any photos or video clips the school or district employees generate for school-based communications—like newsletters, websites, articles for local papers, television programs, and posts to school-monitored social media spaces.

☐ **I give permission for my child's likeness to be used in any school-based communications only when he or she is a part of a larger group of students**—such as athletes on the sidelines of a game, actors in a school performance, or students working together on a project in class.

☐ **I do not give permission** for my child's name or likeness to be used in any school-based communications.

Student name (please print): _____

Homeroom: _____

Parent/guardian name (please print): _____

Signature: _____

Date: _____

CHAPTER 2

Using Social Media Tools to Enhance Professional Development

Like many educators, coauthor and sixth-grade teacher Bill Ferriter is frustrated by traditional approaches to professional development. He states,

> I rarely learn anything useful in professional development sessions simply because the majority of professional development sessions are presented once and never referred to again. What's more, the content covered in professional development sessions never seems to target my own teaching strengths and weaknesses and the structure of professional development sessions never seems to give teachers the opportunity to interact in meaningful ways with one another. As a result, I can't think of too many formal professional development opportunities that have changed who I am as an educator. (Ferriter, 2010a)

Sadly, anyone working in schools will probably find Bill's pessimistic description of professional development all too familiar. Despite the fact that educators passionately argue about the importance of delivering engaging, student-centered lessons built around opportunities for experimentation and social interaction—and despite knowing that ongoing, meaningful professional development is essential to improving teaching and leadership practices (Kostin & Haeger, 2006)—the same passion rarely translates into the work we do to prepare our teachers. Instead, we continue to hire experts to deliver training to large groups of teachers during stand-alone faculty meetings, creating an interesting educational dichotomy: teachers groaning every time they are asked to be learners. Even the euphemisms we use to describe the structure of professional development—Spray and Pray, Sit and Get, Sage on the Stage—are derogatory.

Luckily, researchers have defined the characteristics of effective professional development time and time again. Successful professional development programs consist of structural elements—a connection to curricula, linkages to state and provincial initiatives and certification, integration of information technologies, and use of a variety of instructional strategies—and a strong connection to a school's mission (Peterson, 2002). Quality professional development also promotes reflective practices, fosters collaboration (Browne-Ferrigno & Muth, 2004), focuses on an educator's needs (Marshall, Pritchard, & Gunderson, 2001), is based upon improving student achievement (Haar, 2002), and is embedded and job supported (Lairon & Vidales, 2003). Professional development activities modeled on these characteristics are engaging and meaningful, acting as catalysts for the intrinsic motivation necessary for continued growth.

Principals today are also expected to create team relationships among staff members (Drake & Roe, 2003). Whether they are called professional learning communities, lesson-study groups, action research teams, or communities of practice, collaborative groups of educators growing together are one of the most promising strategies for improving teaching and learning in our schools. As Bill explains, they result in a kind of collective intelligence that can lead to improved practice:

> I've learned to come to planning meetings with my own thinking and lay it on the table, waiting to see what it will become. Sometimes my ideas are taken "as-is" by the group and other times they are discarded completely. Most times, pieces of my thinking are combined and refined with pieces of thinking from the other members of my team, becoming a part of something much bigger—and much better. (Ferriter, 2007)

Finally, mentoring plays a key role in successful professional development (Zepeda, Bengtson, Parylo, Teitelbaum, & Shorner-Johnson, 2008). Mentoring is powerful because it is adaptable to individual career stages (Petzko, 2004), fosters supportive relationships (Peterson & Cosner, 2005), and bridges gaps between educators with various levels of experience (Browne-Ferrigno & Muth, 2004). Even principals need access to mentoring in order to support their school improvement efforts and to revitalize their commitment to creating and sustaining positive learning communities (Foster, Loving, & Shumate, 2000; Evans & Mohr, 1999).

Effective principals understand that improvement in each of these areas—redesigning traditional learning sessions, creating collaborative teams that study instruction together, and providing mentors when appropriate—will have a direct impact on student achievement. The challenge rests in developing holistic models for professional development that are financially responsible, focused on the latest trends in education, and capable of empowering all educators to seek out additional avenues for learning. Luckily, social media spaces provide principals with a cost-effective solution to conveniently deliver and engage in relevant professional development opportunities.

This chapter will discuss how educators can use social media tools like Twitter and Facebook to build personal learning networks, network with peers, acquire knowledge, and digitally attend conferences. Readers will also learn how social media tools can be used to foster reflective practices and enhance mentoring experiences in education, two essential characteristics of high-quality professional development. Our central assertion is that social media tools can enable teachers and principals to differentiate their professional development by focusing on specific areas of personal interest that might not be covered during traditional workshops, seminars, trainings, or conferences.

Twitter as a Tool for Building a Personal Learning Network

A concept that is constantly evolving in professional development forums is that of the personal learning network (PLN). Loosely defined as the human relationships that individuals leverage for learning, PLNs have been around forever, mostly in the form of face-to-face contact among friends, professional colleagues, and family members. In a digital age, however, the Internet and web 2.0 tools—microblogging services, social-networking websites, shared annotation and social book-marking tools, RSS feed readers—have enabled educators to greatly expand their PLNs and to customize their own always-on learning networks.

These 21st century PLNs are built on the professional interests of educators and cultivated through interactions in social media spaces that serve as virtual hubs for consolidating, orga-nizing, discussing, and reflecting on new ideas. PLNs add value to professional growth plans by enabling individuals to take ownership over their own learning. Using new tools, rural principals can reach out to other rural principals for advice on how to best structure collaborative learning teams with small faculties. Using new tools, singleton teachers can find peers teaching similar subjects to plan with for perhaps the first time. Using new tools, teachers working in core class-rooms can introduce their students to new experts and interested audiences.

Twitter is the cornerstone of coauthor Bill Ferriter's digital PLN because it consists of short messages that he can skim easily. "I'm like any other educator," he writes. "I struggle to find time for professional development in my already crowded day. With Twitter, I can read and respond to messages easily from anywhere. Whenever I have a few minutes to spare—between classes, on lunch duty, waiting for flights at the airport, just before going to bed—I'm checking the messages posted by my Twitter network" (Ferriter, 2010a).

And if you spend any time sifting through the messages in Bill's Twitter stream, you will see why he is so drawn to the tool. The users he is following are constantly sharing links to external sourc-es—blog entries, new tools, interesting resources—and are constantly asking provocative ques-tions. Sometimes, conversations develop with several different educators reading and replying to one another. Other times, people are asking for and receiving help. Regardless, every 140-character message has the potential to be a customized learning experience for Bill. As he explains:

> Following people with similar interests—middle school teachers, principals, professors in school leadership, educational technology junkies—means that Twitter serves as a great information filter for me. The kinds of ques-tions being asked and resources being shared are bound to be of interest to me simply because they're being shared by people that care about the same things that I do. (Ferriter, 2010a)

Equally powerful for Bill is the ability to follow the thinking of well-respected educational ex-perts and organizations. Whether it is a high-level policy thinker like Diane Ravitch (http://twitter .com/dianeravitch), a widely recognized instructional technology specialist like Will Richardson (http://twitter.com/willrich45), or a research group churning out influential reports like the Pew

Research Center's Internet and American Life Project (http://twitter.com/pew_internet), they are all posting public messages that any Twitter user can read. Bill writes, "If I gave you the chance to look inside the mind of Diane Ravitch or Will Richardson for a while—to see the websites they're exploring, to answer the questions they're wrestling with, to read what they're writing—you'd take it, wouldn't you? That's what Twitter does for me . . . and it's all instant, asynchronous and free" (Ferriter, 2010a).

Building a digital PLN with Twitter can seem like a daunting task, though. Educators new to Twitter wonder: "Where do I even begin? Whose updates should I follow? What resources can help me find teachers and principals with the same interests and passions as mine?" The good news is that there are many free tools and directories to assist anyone interested in building a digital learning network that suits his or her needs. While most directories contain user-inputted information, others contain lists of educators that Twitter users have vetted. Twitter directories also allow teachers and principals to freely share their own usernames and biographical information— an important step toward being found by others looking to establish digital learning networks. The Twitter homepage and the WeFollow directory are two tools that can help you build your Twitter network.

Twitter Homepage

The most logical place to begin building your Twitter network is on the Twitter homepage (www.twitter.com). After creating a free account and logging in, clicking on the "Who to Follow" link makes it possible to search for other users, browse users by interest categories, and—as your Twitter network grows—view suggestions of educators worth following that Twitter generates after analyzing the networks of the users you are currently following.

WeFollow

Another great place to begin building your Twitter network is the WeFollow website (http://wefollow .com). WeFollow is a directory of Twitter users organized by interests. Typing in an educational tag at the top of the page—education, teacher, principal, teacher trainer, or so on—begins a search on WeFollow. Be prepared to be persistent, though. Sometimes you will have to try different combinations of tags in order to find categories of users that are likely to be of interest to you—and remember that most websites that rely on tagging language eliminate the spaces between tags built from multiple words. That means searching for *elementary school* might not return any results, while searching for *elementaryschool* might return dozens.

As you spend more time in Twitter, building your network will get easier. In the messages that your colleagues share, you will spot new users that are finding great content and asking great questions. Over time, you will also be digitally introduced to users that your peers have chosen to follow, and Twitter will continue to recommend new users to you as your network grows. Finally, you will want to encourage colleagues in your school or district to join you on Twitter. Not only are friendly faces in your Twitter stream a source of encouragement as you tackle new patterns for professional development, colleagues are more likely to read and respond to everything you are sharing. This collective study of common sources with peers you know in person can spark conversations and improve learning beyond the Twitterverse.

Regardless of how you choose to find new people to follow in Twitter, be careful in your selections and quick to *unfollow* people whose messages do not add any value to your own learning. The power of networks is multiplied only when the minds you are looking into are motivated and capable of sharing the kinds of content you care about. Intelligently selecting the right educators for your digital PLN ensures that you will have immediate access to new experiences and insights that can make you a better professional.

Common Patterns of Participation

Understanding the role that Twitter can play in professional development can often be difficult for teachers and principals new to social media spaces. There is something inherently unbelievable about the idea that meaningful learning can take place in streams of 140-character messages. While each user is likely to find different ways to customize their own learning in Twitter, there are six common patterns of participation occurring in most networks: (1) sharing knowledge and resources, (2) monitoring educational news sources, (3) digitally attending important conferences, (4) encouraging reflection, (5) gathering instant feedback, and (6) mentoring colleagues.

Sharing Knowledge and Resources

Twitter has become the go-to source for acquiring relevant information for many teachers and principals. Even users who simply sign up and lurk are learning when they explore the resources others share. Educators using Twitter quickly learn to mine the resources and ideas members of their learning networks share, whether they are confident enough to share or not.

As users become more comfortable with the kinds of conversations that Twitter enables, however, they almost always begin actively participating. By interacting with their networks—sharing URLs, asking questions, offering suggestions—they contribute to the overall health and collective intelligence of their PLN. They also begin to search for streams of conversations directly connected to their work—updates on changing educational policies, examples of instructional practices in action, reviews of new tools and techniques—a process made simple by using the search feature found on the Twitter homepage. For the multitasking, on-the-go educator, the brevity of Twitter messages is ideal, enabling meaningful participation without a significant investment of extra time.

Monitoring Educational News Sources

Many educators also use Twitter to create customized educational newsrooms by adding organizations like the International Society for Technology in Education (http://twitter.com/isteconnects), *Edutopia* (http://twitter.com/edutopia), Scholastic (http://twitter.com/scholastic), and *Education Week* (http://twitter.com/educationweek) to their Twitter streams. Following these organizations provides teachers and principals with a continuous stream of resources connected to current issues and research in the field of education.

Digitally Attending Important Conferences

A growing trend in the educational Twitter community is for teachers and principals to share important thoughts from the sessions that they are attending at popular education conferences. This makes it possible for members of their networks to learn even if they cannot attend professional development sessions in person.

Many conferences and educational events are also starting to utilize *hashtags*—the name for common labels added to the end of Tweets that enable messages to be sorted and searched quickly and easily—to organize specific information related to important presentations, keynotes, or panel discussions. Searching for the common hashtags that conference organizers assign—like #nsdc and #educon—on the Twitter website while a conference is in session makes it possible to easily browse the ideas that other participants are sharing.

Encouraging Reflection

Research on effective teaching over the past two decades has shown that improved practice is linked to inquiry, reflection, and continuous professional growth (Harris, 1998). The goal of education should be habitual reflection and the continual construction of meaning from experiences (York-Barr, Sommers, Ghere, & Montie, 2006). Interestingly enough, Twitter enables all of these behaviors.

As Bill explains, "Some of the most powerful learning experiences I've ever had started with nothing more than a Tweeted question. Inevitably, the members of my network respond—either by adding to my ideas or challenging me to think in a new way. It's this instant intellectual give-and-take that I like the best because I know that my final ideas will be far more polished than anything I started with" (Ferriter, 2010a). For building principals, transparent reflection in Twitter also sends a powerful message to—and provides a powerful model for—their teachers. When principals make themselves intellectually vulnerable in social media spaces, they encourage and enable a school culture that values co-learning and reflection.

Gathering Instant Feedback

As Twitter users become more comfortable with and established in their Twitter networks, they will often turn to Twitter first when they need answers to educational questions. For Bill, this is one of the main benefits of taking the time to create a digital PLN: "It doesn't matter what I need information on—samples of social media policies, new blogs to introduce to my students, links to articles on topics connected to my curricula—my Twitter network can find it for me almost instantly. That saves me a huge amount of time" (Ferriter, 2010a).

Mentoring Colleagues

Despite what we know about the role that mentoring can play in the development of educators, ensuring that every teacher and principal—particularly those working in rural communities or unique content areas—have access to a capable and qualified mentor can be almost impossible for many districts. There just aren't enough resources or mentors to go around.

With Twitter, however, anything is possible. Not only can users reach out to their networks to find resources for struggling peers, they can actively pair their colleagues up with electronic mentors who can provide ongoing support over the course of an entire year. Because a spirit of intellectual philanthropy governs social media spaces, users of almost any service—Twitter, Ning, Facebook, LinkedIn, Diigo—are usually willing to lend a hand to help another educator.

While it is important to note that it can take time to build the kinds of digital relationships that make reflection, instant feedback, and mentoring possible in Twitter—your network is always going to be more likely to support you once they see that you are adding value to the collective intelligence of the group—it is entirely possible for any teacher or principal to develop a powerful network of electronic colleagues to learn with and to rely on using Twitter.

Additional Sources for PLN Building

Principals that embrace the PLN concept as a means of professional growth have the unique opportunity to radically transform the teaching and learning cultures of their schools. Teachers who routinely find little relevance in professional development offerings and in-house trainings can be plugged into self-directed learning opportunities based on their specific interests and needs. For PLNs to be properly implemented and utilized, however, principals must make the time to model the effective use of various social media tools for teachers who may have embraced social media spaces for personal communication, but who have few experiences with using social media spaces to build vibrant communities of co-learners.

While there is no one right collection of tools for developing a 21st century PLN, most educators pair Twitter with one or more of the following social media resources when structuring their own learning networks.

LinkedIn

While originally designed as a tool for businesses to network with potential employees, LinkedIn (www.linkedin.com) has also become a place where educators are finding opportunities to connect with one another. Teachers and principals can join a variety of groups catering to their individual learning interests and can engage in ongoing discussions with other likeminded educators in LinkedIn.

Blogs

Blogs—which are really nothing more than online journals—are incredible sources of information that allow educators to share opinions and have discussions with one another. There are literally thousands of teachers and principals blogging, making this approachable social media tool the perfect medium for reflecting on best practices, finding examples of innovation, and learning from the professional experiences of both novice and veteran educators.

Social Bookmarking and Shared Annotation Services

In their simplest form, social bookmarking services like Diigo (www.diigo.com) offer nothing more than an online place for storing and organizing bookmarked websites. As users become more sophisticated, however—sharing links publicly, adding common tags (short identifying words and phrases) to sort new finds, following sites others have collected, joining groups of users, mining content connected to specific areas of interest, adding public comments to online articles that others can read and respond to—social bookmarking and shared annotation services can become valuable forums for professional growth and reflection.

RSS Readers

Short for "Really Simple Syndication," RSS readers are tools that allow users to keep up with changing content on educational blogs, news sites, wikis, and podcast programs from one web-based homepage. By asking RSS readers to automatically monitor and retrieve new links from individual websites—a process known as *subscribing*—educators can create a customized flow of information that is continually updated and accessible from any Internet-connected device. Instead of visiting twenty different sites to see what's new, RSS feed readers—also known as content aggregators—can automatically organize new updates in one place for you. Popular RSS readers include Google Reader (www.google.com/reader) and RSSOwl (www.rssowl.org).

Wikis

While not as popular as microblogging services like Twitter or social-networking services like Facebook, wikis remain one of the most approachable social media tools. Collaborative websites that allow registered users to create and edit any number of interlinked web pages, wikis encourage information sharing and collaborative learning. Principals can explore exemplary wiki models by visiting Educational Wikis (http://educationalwikis.wikispaces.com) and Wikis in Education (http://wikisineducation.wetpaint.com).

Facebook

Believe it or not, hundreds of teachers and principals are using Facebook to interact with other professionals. The Facebook in Education page (www.facebook.com/education) provides information about how teachers and principals can best use Facebook as a resource. Consider exploring the possibilities of Facebook as a tool for professional development by visiting *Edutopia*'s Facebook page (www.facebook.com/edutopia), where it is always possible to find a provocative conversation or valuable resource on the changing nature of teaching and learning.

Digital Discussion Forums

Consisting of communities of educators interested in similar topics, digital discussion forums are built with social media services that look a lot like Facebook in action. One of the most popular services is Ning (www.ning.com), which enables educators to create or to join specific communities. Ning sites typically offer ongoing discussions, event postings, instant messaging, news articles, and videos. Popular educational Ning sites include the Educator's PLN (http://edupln.com),

Classroom 2.0 (www.classroom20.com), English Companion Ning (http://englishcompanion.ning .com), and Ning in Education (http://education.ning.com).

The lesson to be learned from each of these services is that learning is an inherently social act, a point made in Twitter by educational technology liaison John Pederson when he wrote, "Community building is the new professional development" (ijohnpederson, 2009). Author and eL-earning expert Jay Cross echoes Pederson's ideas:

> Learning is social, and social networks interconnect workers with families, circles of friends, neighborhood groups, professional associations, task teams, business webs, value nets, user groups, flash mobs, gangs, political groups, scout troops, bridge clubs, twelve-step groups, and alumni associations. In one sense, our worker is defined by who he knows. Our definition of learning must embrace the people the worker interacts with and the learning that comes from their interacting with one another. (Cross, 2007, p. 18)

With the right digital tools, anyone can build a community of passionate, likeminded educators committed to improving student achievement through innovative practices. Customized learning is just a click away for teachers and principals willing to develop their own 21st century PLNs.

21st Century PLNs at the District Level

One district working diligently to show teachers how to use social media spaces to build vibrant communities of co-learners is the St. Vrain Valley School District in Longmont, Colorado. Like most school districts, St. Vrain wants to ensure that every student succeeds. Recognizing that ensuring student success depends on a knowledgeable and competent teaching staff committed to innovative practice and peer-to-peer collaboration, the district—under the leadership of instructional technologists Bud Hunt and Michelle Bourgeois—implemented an initiative designed to support teams of teachers who agreed to spend two years studying the impact that new technologies could have on their work with one another and with students. Known as members of the district's first Digital Learning Collaborative (DLC) (http://bit.ly/stvraindlc), the teams consist of eighty teachers from fifteen different schools (Griffin Good & Kalmon, 2010).

DLC team leaders first met with Hunt and Bourgeois in November 2009 to study common collaborative processes and structures (sets of meeting minutes, norms for collaboration, and visual organizers) and common collaborative tools (the district's Virtual Campus, Google Docs, and blogs) that teachers could begin experimenting with. School-based DLC teams began meeting monthly and holding regular online conversations in December 2009. In some schools, these meetings were structured affairs with formal agendas designed to introduce and explore the role that technology could play in instruction. In other schools, these meetings became informal times for experimenting with new tools for teaching and learning. In all cases, though, cohort members were expected to publicly record reflections after each meeting, making their own learning transparent to their peers (Griffin Good & Kalmon, 2010).

Interested in knowing more about the impact that the DLC project was having on the professional learning practices of cohort members, Hunt and Bourgeois asked Dixie Griffin Good and Stevan Kalmon of the Council on 21st Century Learning (www.C21L.org) to study the project and report on their findings. After observing meetings of both school-based cohorts and team leaders and monitoring the online participation patterns of DLC teachers, Griffin Good and Kalmon discovered that introducing new collaborative processes and technologies *can* have a direct impact on instructional practices and teacher learning. Among their specific findings, Griffin Good and Kalmon noted that along with reporting an increased awareness of and comfort level with new technologies, participants in the St. Vrain Valley DLC project almost universally reported increased levels of comfort with collaborative processes and awareness of their own personal learning preferences (Griffin Good & Kalmon, 2010).

Perhaps most importantly, however, Griffin Good and Kalmon discovered that participation in the St. Vrain Valley DLC project had a direct impact on classroom practices. Designed simply to enable teachers to explore new tools and technologies, the first year of the St. Vrain Valley DLC project was not intended to impact instructional practices immediately. What Griffin Good and Kalmon found, however, was that participants were already translating lessons learned in collaborative cohort meetings into their own classroom practices. The opportunity to study alongside colleagues seemed to naturally encourage teachers to experiment with digital tools in their teaching (Griffin Good & Kalmon, 2010).

While levels of participation in school- and district-level electronic conversations were uneven over the course of the St. Vrain DLC project—seven schools had active online discussion forums, while eight saw little interaction in online spaces—contributions picked up toward the end of the first year. For participants new to collaborative technologies, simply mastering new tools was a challenge. Project leaders expect to see increased evidence of the impact of digital networking during year two of the DLC project, as teachers become more aware of what is possible with collaborative technologies and more fluent in implementing them (Griffin Good & Kalmon, 2010).

What is most impressive, though, is that members of St. Vrain Valley's first digital learning cohort appreciated the opportunity to learn about new tools and technologies together. In fact, 95 percent of respondents to an end-of-year survey reported a willingness to recommend the experience to their colleagues (Griffin Good & Kalmon, 2010). That is proof positive that busy teachers can and do appreciate *meaningful* professional development.

Next Steps

For Tom Whitby, adjunct professor of education at St. Joseph's College, the beauty of a digital PLN rests in the ability to build professional relationships with other educators, regardless of their location. "The connectedness of individuals through the ages was always limited by time and distance," he writes. "If people with common interests were available and close by each other, connections could be made. Today, with the digital advantages of technology, people can connect anytime, anywhere crossing time zones and borders. We are no longer just connected locally, or nationally, but globally" (T. Whitby, personal communication, September 4, 2010).

Once you are convinced that you are ready to start building—or helping your teachers to build—the kind of connected network that Whitby describes, consider taking the following steps: explore one tool, formalize a process for documenting the learning, and publicize your efforts.

Explore One Tool

One of the mistakes that educators new to social media spaces and digital PLNs often make is trying to participate in too many conversations all at once. While their intentions are good—joining multiple communities can introduce users to a wider range of viewpoints and perspectives—they quickly become overwhelmed. To ensure that your efforts to integrate digital collaboration into your professional learning practices succeed, choose one social media space at a time to explore, and then lurk for a while.

Monitor the kinds of interactions and opportunities that your chosen space makes possible. Look for familiar professional faces—peers from other districts, leaders in the educational community, and organizations that you trust and respect. Determine just how difficult participating—adding comments, reading content, finding links, and sharing resources—will be in the forum that you are exploring, and consider how well the interactions you are observing align with your personal learning preferences. Consider monitoring some educators you know or those suggested in the handout "Common Patterns of Participation on Twitter" (page 45).

Once you find a social media space that seems like a good fit, jump right in and start networking. The more you practice—both with the tools you have chosen and the communication patterns necessary for connecting with others digitally—the more comfortable you will be learning with your 21st century PLN. A list of starting points spotlighting great educational conversations happening in a wide variety of social media spaces is included in the handout "Exploring Educational Conversations in Social Media Spaces" (page 47).

Formalize a Process for Documenting the Learning

For many educators, participating in social media spaces seems like nothing more than a waste of time because few schools and districts officially recognize digital collaboration as meaningful professional development. They wonder, "Why should I spend time building a digital PLN if I'm not going to be given any professional growth credits for the learning I'm doing there?"

Addressing this hesitance requires principals and district-level leaders to formalize a process for documenting the impact that collaborative online learning is having on professional growth, something that can start with the handout "Tracking the Impact of Social Media Spaces on Professional Development" (page 52). Formalizing a process for documenting the learning being done in social media spaces can give supervisors a measure of assurance that their employees are choosing growth opportunities that carry value for both the individual and the organization.

Publicize Your Efforts

Conversations around school leadership in the past decade have focused on the idea that principals should be the instructional leaders of their schools. Instructional leadership, however, is difficult for principals to demonstrate to their entire faculties, because it is almost impossible for a school leader to find the time to engage in deep and meaningful conversations about instruction with every colleague every day. This unfortunate isolation can lead to teachers who openly question the ability of their principal to lead in the areas of curriculum and instruction.

Once you start to interact in social media spaces, however—commenting on blogs, posting messages on Twitter, and joining in the discussions happening on Nings—your ideas become transparent to everyone. Share this work with your faculties. Let them know where they can find you thinking online. Encourage them to interact with you electronically. Doing so will not only result in more teachers who are interested in building digital PLNs, it will result in more teachers who are aware of just what you know and can do—both with technology and with the meaty ideas necessary for serving as an instructional leader.

In a 2007 interview, Nicholas Negroponte, the director of the Massachusetts Institute of Technology's Media Lab, bemoaned the state of technology integration in schools. He wrote, "In fact, one of the saddest but most common conditions in elementary school computer labs (when they exist in the developing world), is the children are being trained to use Word, Excel and PowerPoint. I consider that criminal, because children should be making things, communicating, exploring, sharing, not running office automation tools" (as cited in "Low-Cost Laptop," 2007). It is difficult, however, to be surprised by slowly changing instructional practices in classrooms simply because little has changed in the way that our teachers use technology to learn.

Working as hard as they can, teachers draw from well-worn bags of tricks in an honest attempt to prepare their students for tomorrow. Incorporating social media spaces into professional growth plans, however, might just lead to a digital revolution in our classrooms. As teachers explore the ways that collaborative technologies can make their own learning more efficient and effective, they are likely to pass those practices on to their students—a change today's students will undeniably benefit from.

Common Patterns of Participation on Twitter

It can be difficult to believe that meaningful professional development can actually occur in Twitter, a social media service that limits messages to 140 characters. To build confidence in the value of joining the Twitterverse, for a few weeks, consider monitoring the messages that any educator using Twitter is posting, and then complete this handout.

Type of educator you will monitor: _____

Name of educator: _____

Dates of monitoring: _____

(Feel free to choose any educator using Twitter whose work better mirrors your own. Include his or her name, a direct link to his or her Twitter stream, and a short description of his or her professional work.)

Looking for suggestions? Consider following the streams of one of the following educators.

Nicholas Provenzano (http://twitter.com/thenerdyteacher): High school English teacher with interests in the classroom integration of technology

Eric Townsley (http://twitter.com/erictownsley): Middle school principal in Iowa with interests in educational technology, school leadership, assessment, and pedagogy

Steven Anderson (http://twitter.com/web20classroom): Instructional technologist at a middle school in North Carolina with interests in the role that social media can play in teaching and learning

Nancy Blair (http://twitter.com/blairteach): School improvement consultant with interests in middle grades education, English and language arts, and literacy.

Types of Activities Observed
(Check all that apply.)

☐ Sharing knowledge and resources

☐ Monitoring educational news sources

☐ Tracking important conferences

☐ Encouraging reflection

☐ Gathering instant feedback

☐ Mentoring colleagues

☐ Other: _____

Frequency of Posting

☐ About once a week

☐ About once a day

☐ Several times per day

Questions to Consider

1. What trends do you notice in the patterns of participation for the educator that you've been monitoring? Are certain behaviors more common than others? Are there certain behaviors that seem more valuable to you than others? Which ones? Why?

2. Did you learn any lessons that will be valuable in your primary work while monitoring the Twitter stream of this educator? What were they? How did this information help you do your job better or make your work easier?

3. Did you learn any lessons about networking in social media spaces while monitoring the Twitter stream of this educator? What were they?

4. What questions about common patterns of communication on Twitter do you still have? What excites you about building your own network on Twitter?

5. How do you intend to build on this learning experience? Will you study the Twitter streams of additional educators? Are you ready to start your own Twitter account?

Exploring Educational Conversations in Social Media Spaces

Successfully developing a 21st century PLN depends on choosing a social media space that aligns with your personal learning preferences, provides access to information that can improve your work, and connects you to colleagues that you can learn from. Before committing to any social media space, consider checking out a few of the following conversations and determining how likely they are to be a good fit for you.

Self-Assessment

Before exploring any social media space, it is important to take a few moments to reflect on your own personal learning preferences and to think through what you're most hoping to learn from a 21st century PLN.

How do you learn best? *(Check all that apply.)*

☐ By writing and reflecting

☐ By watching videos demonstrating practice in action

☐ By joining ongoing conversations with colleagues

☐ By reading content—like books, articles, and online sources—connected to my work

☐ By sharing what I know with others

☐ By sitting in on experts' formal presentations

☐ Other: _____

How much time do you have for learning?

☐ Less than 60 minutes per week

☐ 60–90 minutes per week

☐ 90–120 minutes per week

☐ Over 120 minutes per week

What devices are you likely to use to connect to your PLN? *(Check all that apply.)*

☐ My computer

☐ My mobile phone

☐ My iPad

☐ My iPod touch

☐ Other: _____

Spend a few minutes writing about what you would like to see happening in the social media spaces that you embrace. What kinds of resources would you like to find there? What would make your work instantly easier and more rewarding? Why do these things matter to you?

Social Media Starting Points for Educators

The following sites are home to some of the most popular and engaging conversations taking place between educators in social media spaces. Choose a few to explore, and then decide how well each tool aligns with your own personal learning preferences and behaviors.

Twitter

The following links connect to strands of conversations happening in Twitter.

Communicating and Connecting With Social Media © 2011 Solution Tree Press • solution-tree.com
Visit **go.solution-tree.com/technology** to download this page.

Ed Chat

http://bit.ly/twittertag1

One of the most common tags attached to educators' Twitter posts is #edchat. This link connects to the constant stream of resources being shared with the #edchat tag.

Connected Principals Chat

http://bit.ly/twittertag2

Another popular Twitter tag is #cpchat. Principals interested in connecting with and supporting each other use it.

Which statements describe this social media space?
(Check all that apply.)

☐ I found links to valuable resources here.

☐ I was challenged by interesting questions and ideas here.

☐ I was not intimidated by the time commitment that participating here is likely to require.

☐ I was surprised by how valuable this social media space seemed to be.

☐ I'll be able to access this social media space from my mobile phone.

☐ This social media space seems to be a good fit for me.

☐ Other: _____

What are the strengths and weaknesses of this social media space?

How well does this social media space align with your own personal learning preferences?

LinkedIn

While you'll have to sign up for a free LinkedIn account to access them, the following links connect to strands of conversations happening between educators on LinkedIn.

Education Innovators

http://linkd.in/eduinnovate

This strand of conversation brings together principals, teachers, and professional development providers interested in innovation in education.

Web 2.0 Group

http://linkd.in/web20group

This strand of conversation brings together a group of educational professionals interested in studying the role that collaborative technologies can play in teaching and learning.

Which statements describe this social media space?
(Check all that apply.)

☐ I found links to valuable resources here.

☐ I was challenged by interesting questions and ideas here.

☐ I was not intimidated by the time commitment that participating here is likely to require.

☐ I was surprised by how valuable this social media space seemed to be.

☐ I'll be able to access this social media space from my mobile phone.

☐ This social media space seems to be a good fit for me.

☐ Other: _____

What are the strengths and weaknesses of this social media space?

How well does this social media space align with your own personal learning preferences?

Blogs

While there are thousands of blogs that you might consider exploring, these might serve as a good starting point for learning how blogs become social spaces.

Dangerously Irrelevant

http://bit.ly/blogsample1

The blog of Scott McLeod, professor of educational leadership at Iowa State University, Dangerously Irrelevant is a constant source of provocative questions, valuable resources, and good conversations.

Weblogg-Ed

http://weblogg-ed.com

The blog of Will Richardson, Weblogg-Ed is constantly exploring the changing nature of teaching and learning in the 21st century.

(Visit http://education.alltop.com to find additional educational blogs worth exploring.)

Which statements describe this social media space?
(Check all that apply.)

☐ I found links to valuable resources here.

☐ I was challenged by interesting questions and ideas here.

☐ I was not intimidated by the time commitment that participating here is likely to require.

☐ I was surprised by how valuable this social media space seemed to be.

☐ I'll be able to access this social media space from my mobile phone.

☐ This social media space seems to be a good fit for me.

☐ Other: _____

What are the strengths and weaknesses of this social media space?

How well does this social media space align with your own personal learning preferences?

Ning

The following links connect to two of the most vibrant Ning networks for educators, which you can explore after creating a free user account.

Classroom 2.0

www.classroom20.com

Perhaps the largest and best known Ning for educators, Classroom 2.0 is a virtual home for anyone interested in learning more about the role that social media can play in education.

English Companion Ning

http://englishcompanion.ning.com

A great example of how content-area teachers are creating customized social-networking spaces to learn together, the English Companion Ning won the Edublogs award for Best Educational Use of a Social Networking Service in 2009.

Which statements describe this social media space?
(Check all that apply.)

☐ I found links to valuable resources here.

☐ I was challenged by interesting questions and ideas here.

☐ I was not intimidated by the time commitment that participating here is likely to require.

☐ I was surprised by how valuable this social media space seemed to be.

☐ I'll be able to access this social media space from my mobile phone.

☐ This social media space seems to be a good fit for me.

☐ Other: _____

What are the strengths and weaknesses of this social media space?

How well does this social media space align with your own personal learning preferences?

Diigo

Built around the collective sharing of web-based resources, Diigo enables users to form groups and extend conversations on focused topics of interest.

Diigo Education Groups List

http://bit.ly/diigoedugroups

This link connects to the master list of education groups that have already been formed in Diigo. Here, you'll find groups collectively studying and sharing resources around everything from the use of instructional technology in literacy classrooms to teachers studying Japanese manga together.

Which statements describe this social media space?
(Check all that apply.)

☐ I found links to valuable resources here.

☐ I was challenged by interesting questions and ideas here.

☐ I was not intimidated by the time commitment that participating here is likely to require.

☐ I was surprised by how valuable this social media space seemed to be.

☐ I'll be able to access this social media space from my mobile phone.

☐ This social media space seems to be a good fit for me.

☐ Other: _____

What are the strengths and weaknesses of this social media space?

How well does this social media space align with your own personal learning preferences?

Tracking the Impact of Social Media Spaces on Professional Development

Some of the best professional development opportunities for educators take place as a result of interactions in social media spaces. These interactions, however, rarely count toward requirements for license renewal simply because they are not carefully documented. Consider using this form over the course of the next year to record the impact that interactions in social media spaces are having on your own professional growth.

Title of activity: _____

(If this activity was not a formal experience with a defined title, generate a generic title that can be used to refer to this activity in our conversations about your professional growth.)

General Information

Type of Activity

☐ Video conference

☐ Online course

☐ Twitter conversation

☐ Social bookmarking

☐ Shared annotation

☐ Wiki creation

☐ Facebook interaction

☐ Blog reading, writing, or commenting

☐ Other: _____

Date(s) activity occurred: _____

(If this activity is a part of a longer conversation, include a starting and ending date for your work.)

Time invested: _____

(Please estimate the amount of time that you've invested in this activity and any follow-up work done as a result of new ideas that you've learned. Be prepared to justify your estimate when your primary evaluator asks.)

Links to Online Evidence of Your Participation in This Activity

(This can include links to Twitter messages or posts in digital forums. It can also include links to comments left on—or entries written for—blogs. Remember to use link shorteners like http://bit.ly or http://snipurl.com to make sharing links to online evidence manageable.)

Questions to Consider

Briefly describe the nature of this professional learning experience.

1. How did this learning experience connect to our school's mission and vision statements?

2. How did this learning experience connect to your own personal growth plans? Why was this learning experience important to you as an educator? How will it change who you are as a teacher or principal?

3. How has this learning experience impacted the work you do with the teachers you supervise, the colleagues you collaborate with, or the students in your classrooms?

4. How do you intend to build on this learning experience? Will there be additional studies involved? Are you planning new lessons as a result of what you've learned? Can you share what you've learned with other teachers on our faculty?

Communicating and Connecting With Social Media © 2011 Solution Tree Press • solution-tree.com
Visit **go.solution-tree.com/technology** to download this page.

3

Developing Professionally Responsible Social Media Practices

As we have seen in the first two chapters, using social media to communicate with constituents and connect with colleagues in new digital spaces is gaining traction with a wider audience of school leaders, experts, and educational organizations. Negative stories trumpeted by media outlets, however, continue to slow adoption. It is difficult to expect educators to completely embrace services like Twitter and Facebook when they are constantly surrounded with headlines like, "Teacher Loses Job After Commenting About Students, Parents on Facebook" (Heussner & Fahmy, 2010).

As a result, the majority of schools and districts are overly cautious about the role that digital spaces can play in their own communication and professional development plans. As coauthor Jason Ramsden, chief technology officer for Ravenscroft School in Raleigh, North Carolina, explains, "I understand the excitement *and* hesitation that comes with conversations about using social media in our schools. In my experience, most educators think social media means social networking on Facebook. While Facebook is certainly one tool that can be used, there are many other tools available, each with its own set of positive and negative factors that need to be considered" (Ramsden, 2009).

Complicating matters is the fact that—just as educators are struggling to find the proper balance between professional transparency and the protection of privacy as they work and play online—schools and districts are struggling with what it means to have employees interacting as individuals, learners, and leaders in social media spaces. "Online technology has outpaced our laws and policies," explains Richie Escovedo, spokesperson for the Mansfield Independent School District in Texas (as cited in Fox, 2010). This reality is made more challenging by three factors: (1) the wide range of interactions enabled by ever-changing digital tools and services, (2) the increasing sophistication of tech-savvy workforces, and (3) the impossible challenge of monitoring the actions of large numbers of teachers and students working beyond the schoolhouse walls. Larry

Shaw, the executive director of the United Educators Association, notes, "Ninety-nine percent of our teachers mean well, but it's that 1 percent that ruins it for everyone" (as cited in Fox, 2010).

Individual schools and districts are approaching these challenges differently. Beginning in the 2010–2011 school year, the Lee County School District—one of Florida's largest, serving the Fort Myers area—implemented a social media policy that specifically prohibits teachers from communicating with students on any social-networking site (Lytle, 2010; see the policy at http://bit.ly /leecounty). Hoping to engage students while simultaneously ensuring that the boundaries of online relationships between students and teachers are clearly defined, other districts (like the Salt Lake City, Utah, Granite School District) are providing structured opportunities for teachers and students to collaborate in school-monitored social media spaces (n.a., 2010).

In school systems without formal social media policies (like the Wake County Public Schools, North Carolina's largest district), administrators point to existing codes of ethics for teachers, arguing that they apply to interactions in social media spaces as well (Hui, 2010). A similar practice governs teachers and students at Rutgers Preparatory School, a private school in Somerset, New Jersey. As John H. Miller, the Rutgers Prep middle school principal, details, "We have a 'Statement of Ethics and Values' explaining that teachers' and students' behavior online should mirror their words and actions on campus" (J. Miller, personal communication, September 5, 2010).

While many district-level leaders worry about maintaining boundaries between personal and professional lives in social media spaces, Jason points out that the lines between the personal and professional lives of educators have always been blurred. "Consider the days when a beloved teacher or respected principal was well known through their involvement in the local community," he writes. "The many eyes of that community were watching then as well. When it comes to using social media, though, our actions are infinitely more visible and permanent. That means the line between our personal and professional lives is not only blurred, it is also incredibly fragile" (Ramsden, 2010).

Blurred and *fragile*—key terms to remember when planning to enter social media spaces—are often at the center of school-based social media controversies. Consider the story of David Telesca, the former superintendent of schools for the Windsor Locks School District in Connecticut whose Facebook comments started a local firestorm that ended up costing Telesca his job.

A lifelong educator, Telesca moved from the classroom to the front office, first as an assistant principal, then as a principal, and finally as the assistant superintendent for Plainville Community Schools in Plainville, Connecticut. Telesca reached the top of education's professional ladder when he was installed as the superintendent for the Windsor Locks Schools, a small suburban district located eleven miles north of Hartford, Connecticut.

On July 1, 2010—the first day of Telesca's tenure as superintendent and a day when the Windsor Locks School District was closed—he noted on his Facebook page that he "slept until 10 a.m." and then "browsed the Internet." He later quipped, "If every day is like this, it'll be the best job ever." During an exchange of comments with friends between July 1 and July 9 about how his new role would not always be so easy, Telesca posted that his first day in the office involved "counseling an administrator to retire or face termination" which was followed by the emoticon for smiling (as cited in Beals, 2010a).

On September 14, 2010, faced with growing community dissatisfaction, Telesca resigned from his position as part of a settlement with the school board over his Facebook posts. "The board felt as though the recent disclosure on a Facebook posting regarding a school district personnel matter damaged Mr. Telesca's credibility at a critical juncture in his superintendency," explained Windsor Locks School Board Chairwoman Patricia King (as cited in Beals 2010b). While stories like Telesca's are part of today's social media landscape, remembering that our lives are public by default is essential to success. Jason notes, "As educators, it is important to remember that our right to free speech is limited by public perception" (Ramsden, 2010).

The good news is that as educators, school leaders, and districts grapple with the constantly changing landscape surrounding social media in schools, teachers and principals can successfully integrate new spaces into their work without taking unusual risks, as long as they get acquainted with—and understand the possible pitfalls of—the tools they are embracing. Preparation is the key, and that preparation comes in the form of key decisions educators must make as they enter social media spaces.

In this chapter, we will explore those decisions and review their impact. Next, we will provide a set of guidelines and good practices for participating in personal learning networks and reaching out to stakeholders in social media spaces. Finally, we will outline important next steps that will help you establish social media plans for yourself and for your schools.

The Social Media Forest

Whether you plan to use social media for your own professional development or to communicate with your school community, stepping into new online spaces is not something to be taken lightly. You will have to think through the personal and professional consequences of living out a life in front of a digital audience. While the balance can be tricky, it is possible for teachers and principals to separate who they are as individuals and as educators online.

The first key decision you will need to make is how tightly you want to connect your personal and professional selves in online spaces. Patrick Larkin, the principal of Burlington High School in Burlington, Massachusetts, believes that tying his online identity closely to his position was a logical choice. "I guess I look at myself as a representative of my school first and then the individual recognition comes second," explains Larkin. "As long as good things are happening for my school then I am happy" (P. Larkin, personal communication, September 12, 2010).

As a result, Larkin's Twitter stream (http://twitter.com/bhsprincipal) and primary blog (www .burlingtonhigh.blogspot.com) are branded with details about his current role. Visitors to both sites will inevitably tie Larkin's ideas and actions online to his building and to his school community. While this carries very real consequences for Larkin—personal sharing on topics unconnected to teaching and learning may not be well received by every audience—it also carries tangible rewards. "I think that it is important for others to see, both in our community and outside of it, that Burlington High School has a presence well beyond our school walls and our town boundary," writes Larkin. "It is vitally important to me that our students, staff, and community start to see the importance of this connection" (P. Larkin, personal communication, September 12, 2010).

Larkin's decision to tie his online identity to his school also makes it possible for Burlington High's online communications to continue even after Larkin moves on. His Twitter username—@bhsprincipal—and his blog name—Burlington HS Principal's Blog—can both be transferred to his successor, creating consistency in the work that his school is doing in social media spaces. While Larkin will need to rebuild his own online presence after he leaves his current position, the communication patterns he is establishing now will remain in place long after he is gone, keeping parents and community members informed without interruption.

For other principals—like Jonathan E. Martin, head of St. Gregory College Preparatory School in Tucson, Arizona—it is a more comfortable decision to separate personal lives from their positions when working in new digital spaces. Creating online identities that are not directly tied to official positions essentially broadens the scope of the communications they can share. As Martin notes, while he is proud of his building and his position—both are shared freely in all of the social networks he has joined—that pride does not mean his online communications are always going to be connected to the work he is doing in his school. He writes, "My Head of School blog (http://21k12blog.net) is more the blog of a head of school, rather than the St. Gregory School Head's Blog. My twitter account (http://twitter.com/JonathanEMartin) is the same. I don't, quite intentionally, call either my blog or my twitter account 'St. Gregory Head's Blog' or @StGregory'sHead" (J. Martin, personal communication, September 4, 2010).

While Martin recognizes the potential in creating permanent, unchanging user accounts that can be maintained even after school leaders change—a choice Patrick Larkin has made by selecting @bhsprincipal as his online identity—he believes that the consequences of creating communication patterns that stakeholders grow to expect but that new administrators are unwilling to maintain can be disastrous for a school community. "I know how easy it is to lose your job or to change jobs," he writes. "As a result, I think we need to be branding ourselves individually even as . . . we use the platform to advocate for our school" (J. Martin, personal communication, September 4, 2010).

Coauthor Eric Sheninger has taken a more blended approach to crafting his online identity. Committed to using social media spaces like Twitter and Facebook to create an online presence for his school, his Twitter account (http://twitter.com/nmhs_principal) identifies him as a representative of—and ties him closely to—his school. However, Eric also maintains a blog (http://esheninger.blogspot.com) that is not directly connected to the work he is doing at New Milford High. He explains, "It's my hope that the New Milford High School principal will always be sharing in Twitter and Facebook, building on the presence that I'm currently creating in both spaces. But I also want to create a professional presence for myself that I can take with me when I move into new roles" (Sheninger, 2010b).

The following questions can help you to determine whether tying yourself closely to your school or representing yourself as an individual in online spaces is the right choice for your current situation.

What Is Your Primary Goal for Entering Social Media Spaces?

As we have outlined throughout *Communicating and Connecting With Social Media*, educators are using new digital spaces to reach out to key stakeholders and to pursue differentiated professional development. While both of these purposes are equally valuable, clarifying your *primary* purpose for integrating social-networking tools into your work can help you to determine whether tying yourself to your school or entering new spaces as an individual is the right choice.

If reaching out to stakeholders is the most important outcome, consider creating an identity branded with the name of your school or position. Doing so will make it easier to identify your work as an official source of school-based information. If you are more interested in using social media spaces to improve your own professional learning, consider entering social media spaces as an individual. Doing so will ensure that any messages that you share unrelated to specific school happenings do not leave your stakeholders confused.

Does Your District Allow You the Freedom to Express Your Thoughts and Ideas on Education?

Chances are your school district already has clear communication policies in place. These policies—often built upon a district's determination to craft and coordinate messaging efforts—will play a significant role in your choice to tie yourself closely to your school or to develop an individual presence in online spaces.

If your district allows you the freedom to express your thoughts as their representative, consider setting up your social media accounts under the name of your official position. Doing so creates communication patterns that will outlive your tenure in your current school. If your district carefully coordinates messages, however, you should consider creating user accounts that identify you as an individual instead of as the leader of your school. Doing so can prevent embarrassing situations where you communicate messages that do not neatly align with the district's stated direction and core beliefs.

Will Your Successors Use Social Media Tools?

Another important factor to consider when choosing whether to represent your school or yourself as an individual online is the general attitude toward social media spaces in your district. If the idea of creating a presence in social media spaces highly motivates your senior leaders and colleagues in other schools, chances are your successors will gladly build on your initial efforts and be interested in inheriting user accounts closely tied to your school.

On the other hand, if there is a general hesitance toward using social media spaces for communication and professional development in your district, tying your accounts closely to your school could harm your community when new leaders fail to maintain the presence that you have developed online. In these situations, establishing yourself as an individual in the social networks that you are exploring is a more responsible decision for both you and your organization.

How Important Is Sharing in Areas Outside of Education?

The final and most important factor in your decision to tie your accounts closely to your school or to establish yourself as an individual in online spaces is your own personal interests and enthusiasms. If you find that your passion for your school and for topics connected to education is your primary interest, then tying your accounts closely to your school is not only a safe decision, it can maximize the effort that you invest in building a presence in social media spaces. Not only will you enjoy the time that you spend interacting with likeminded peers online, you will be promoting your school and communicating with stakeholders at the same time.

If you are equally motivated by using social media tools to build relationships and to share ideas beyond education, however, your best bet is to enter new digital spaces as an individual. While using social media tools to share information about faith, family, personal interests, and political affiliations is perfectly acceptable for individuals, it is an irresponsible practice for educators who have tied their online identities to their schools. You may want to consider adding disclaimers to your public profiles in social media spaces noting that your views are your own and not those of your employer—especially when blogging or tweeting about education. Finally, if you are particularly concerned about potential conflicts between your personal ideas and the positions of your district, you can always use the security features in social media spaces to make your messaging private and available only to people who you specifically grant access to. Doing so, however, should be a last resort because it will significantly impact your ability to take advantage of the collective wisdom of the thousands of educators who are already networking in popular social media spaces.

Before you start working in online spaces, be sure to spend time talking through your decision with colleagues who have already embraced social-networking tools for communication or professional development. Doing so will help you find an approach—tying your online identity to your school, entering social media spaces as an individual, or adopting a blended model of participation—that is right for you.

Guidelines and Good Practices for Participating in Social Media Spaces

Once you have chosen an approach for entering social media spaces that matches your individual goals and personal style, it is essential to think through the kinds of guidelines and good practices that can keep your efforts to interact online productive and professionally safe. Start by running your plans past your immediate supervisors. Fear is often the driving force in conversations about integrating social media spaces into education, and it is entirely possible that you will run into this reality as your bosses become aware of your efforts to use new digital tools for communication and professional development.

Overcoming these fears begins and ends by keeping your supervisors informed about what you are doing online. Consider sharing links to the conversations you have started or joined in social media spaces. You should also be able to demonstrate how social-networking services are enabling new interactions with stakeholders and changing the way you learn. Remember, it is your responsibility to help your supervisors understand why social media spaces matter—and understanding always begins with awareness.

It is also important to remember that even if you have chosen to enter social media spaces as an individual, others are still likely to see you as a representative of your school and your district. Separating your online identity from your formal position does not automatically separate you from the work you have chosen to do each day. That's why consistently respecting district policies and programs in your online communications is so important. While it is unlikely that you will agree with every decision senior leaders of your system make, publicly questioning those decisions online can create ill will in the central office, confuse the stakeholders who have chosen to follow your messages, and damage your system's credibility in the eyes of your community.

One of the most difficult shifts for educators new to social media spaces is recognizing that online communications are instantly permanent, replicable, and public. Anything you inadvertently share—links to inappropriate sites, off-color comments about kids or communities, expressions of frustration with the capacity of your colleagues, controversial opinions on hot-button issues—become a part of an ongoing conversation that you no longer control once you press *send*. Messages that you may have intended for individual members of your growing digital network can quickly spread, reaching audiences you didn't even know you had.

That means you have to think twice about the kinds of content you are choosing to create and the people you are choosing to interact with. When you decide to enter social media spaces, you are deciding to introduce a once unimaginable amount of transparency into your life. Safely living with that transparency depends on remembering that nothing you do online is private. Training yourself to see your personal life as something lived beyond the keyboard can help prevent the kinds of inadvertent comments that ruin reputations and careers.

Creating profiles in popular social-networking services also means that you will be spending far more time interacting with parents and students than ever before. Chances are your students will be excited to find you in the spaces they have embraced. They will pepper you with questions, comments, complaints, and calls for help with classwork. Parents will look for clarification on school policies and procedures—and members of both groups are likely to interact with you in ways that are far less formal than you are used to.

While these kinds of actions are not unusual—social media sites are still predominately casual places where people are networking with family and friends—you have to maintain professional relationships with parents and students at all times. Remember, you may be the first educator that your parents and students have ever encountered online. That means you are modeling the kinds of digital communication patterns that are appropriate between schools and the stakeholders they serve. Slip into the kinds of informal discourse common between peers in social media spaces, and you will inevitably damage your professional standing in the eyes of the very people you are trying to lead.

Finally, remember that regardless of whether you tie your online identity closely to your school or enter social media spaces as an individual, those who follow your messages are going to want to know a bit about who you are as a person. Sharing individual successes or updates about what is new in your own life can help your audience feel connected to you and can add authenticity to your online work.

Keep in mind, however, that your online persona should be a reflection of the role that you have chosen to play. If you are messaging in social media spaces as the leader of your school, you will want to make sure that 95 percent of the content you share is directly connected to the work the teachers, students, and stakeholders of your school community are doing. If you have entered social media spaces as an individual, a balance of 70 percent professional content and 30 percent personal content is more appropriate and engaging.

There is no doubt that schools and districts are going to need sets of structures and guidelines for teachers and principals interested in using social media spaces for communication and professional development. It is not just reasonable but professionally responsible to define acceptable patterns of participation and to outline the expectations that your organization holds for employees using digital tools. The risk, however, is that fears will result in overly restrictive policies that paralyze innovative educators from truly taking advantage of new services.

That's why sets of suggested practices are so valuable. Not only can they keep you safe as an individual working in social media spaces, they can also provide a general framework for policies that you implement for your faculties. While they should be detailed enough to provide guidance in how to best integrate social media spaces into the professional lives of educators, they should also be general enough to encourage innovation. Develop your own set of practices, and share them with your most motivated teachers. Then, watch as they use social media spaces to change the work they are doing with one another, with their parents, and with their students. Before long, they will be spreading best practices built on responsible guidelines throughout your organization.

Next Steps

The point we are trying to make is that participating in social media spaces can be both safe *and* rewarding for educators who are willing to make a few key decisions and to define a few good practices worth following. That process begins by developing a plan, crafting an exit strategy, and creating districtwide social media policies and guidelines.

Developing a Plan

As in any new experience, educators who embrace social media spaces are often consumed with energy and excitement. That energy and excitement—reinforced by relationships with likeminded digital peers—can often lead to careless practices. Bridling this enthusiasm is best done by planning your participation in social media spaces. Thinking through the kinds of choices that are appropriate for your current position—a process supported by the "Planning Your Participation in Social Media Spaces" handout (page 64)—can ensure that poor choices do not put you into professional jeopardy.

Crafting an Exit Strategy

Crafting an exit strategy is a critically important yet often overlooked step for educational leaders entering social media spaces as representatives of their school communities. If this is the social media approach you choose to adopt, you should work to ensure that communications continue after you have left your current position. That process starts by making sure the tools and services you choose can be easily transferred to those who come after you. Your exit strategy should also include logistical preparations (providing usernames and passwords for every service), philosophical preparations (sharing the rationale for posting patterns and explaining the types of messaging your community has come to expect), and professional development preparations (allotting time to train those who come after you). A good exit strategy can ensure a smooth and uninterrupted flow of information to your school's stakeholders once you have moved on to a new role in your system.

Creating Districtwide Social Media Policies and Guidelines

While the primary focus of this chapter was preparing yourself for safe participation in social media spaces, your school and district are probably also thinking through systemic policies outlining the behaviors they expect from employees living and working online. As you become more comfortable in social media spaces, we hope you will play a role in crafting these guidelines.

As counterintuitive as it may seem, studying the characteristics of good social media practices for your school or district requires turning to the private sector and learning from businesses with extensive experience in new digital spaces. Radian6, a company formed in 2006 to help businesses harness the power of new media conversations, has created a simple template (http://bit.ly /socialmediapolicybasics) for developing effective social media guidelines that can provide a solid foundation for any district-based effort. You might also consider exploring the database of social media policy samples (http://bit.ly/socialmediapolicysamples) maintained by Chris Boudreaux at the Social Media Governance website.

Whenever you feel like social media practices are leaving you and your school or district at risk, remember the warning of Marisa Peacock, a social media strategist and marketing consultant who blogs for several sites, including edSocialMedia (www.edsocialmedia.com):

> Social media is about transparency, and transparency is about getting a naked look at what really goes on. In order for it to work successfully, a school has to have confidence in its faculty, students, parents and alumnae [*sic*]. It has to trust that the school is worth promoting, directly or indirectly. Instead of worrying about the message your school is sending on social media platforms, consider the message your school is sending by NOT engaging with social media at all. (Peacock, 2010)

Planning Your Participation in Social Media Spaces

While participating in social media spaces can be initially intimidating for educators, carefully thinking through several key decisions and setting several good practices for yourself in advance can help make your work personally rewarding and professionally safe. Consider using this handout to begin planning your participation in social media spaces.

Key Decision

Decide whether to tie your online identity to your school or position or enter social media spaces as an individual.

For any educator, one of the most important initial decisions is whether to tie his or her online identity to his or her current school or position (the choice Patrick Larkin made when he selected @bhsprincipal as his Twitter identity and Burlington High School Principal's Blog as his blog name) or to enter social media spaces as an individual (the choice Jonathan Martin made when he chose @jonathanemartin as his Twitter identity and 21K12 as his blog name). Check the following statements that best describe your current position and your intentions for entering social media spaces. The column with the most checks will indicate which choice is right for you.

Tying Your Online Identity to Your Current School or Position

☐ My primary interest in entering social media spaces is to learn more about educational topics.

☐ I am comfortable being seen as an educator first and an individual second by members of my school community.

☐ I care deeply about modeling social media behaviors for the members of my school community.

☐ I care deeply about building an online presence for our school that stretches beyond the borders of our community.

☐ My school community is active in social media spaces.

☐ My school community is critical of our school's current communication plan.

☐ My district allows me to freely share thoughts and ideas on education as its representative.

☐ Creating patterns of communication that can outlive my tenure in my current position is important to me.

☐ My successor is likely to continue communicating with important stakeholders in social media spaces.

Entering Social Media Spaces as an Individual

☐ While I'm interested in using social media spaces to learn more about educational topics, I'm equally interested in using social media spaces to keep in touch with my family and to pursue areas of personal interest beyond education.

☐ I want to build a social media presence that I can take with me when I move to a new position or role in education.

☐ My school community is not particularly active in social media spaces.

☐ My school community is satisfied with our school's current communication plan.

☐ My district has yet to embrace social media spaces.

☐ My district carefully coordinates messaging efforts and discourages employees from expressing individual positions on educational topics.

☐ It is unlikely that the successor to my current position will embrace social media spaces or continue building on the presence I begin.

Good Practices and Patterns for Participation

It is equally important for educators entering social media spaces to develop good online practices that are customized for their current situation. Answering the following questions can help you do just that.

One of the first steps that you've got to take in order to keep your participation in social media spaces professionally safe is to keep your supervisors aware of what you're doing online.

1. Which individuals in your system do you need to reach out to? What will be their initial reactions to your decision to join conversations in social media spaces? Why?

2. What evidence can you use to demonstrate the benefits of using social media spaces for communication and professional development?

It is equally important that you respect district policies and programs in your online communications. Being overly critical will anger members of your central office and leave your school's stakeholders confused.

1. Which policies and programs is your district most invested in? How does the general community feel about these policies and programs? How likely is it that your stakeholders will share criticisms with you about these policies and programs in social media spaces?

2. Which programs will it be difficult for you to be positive about in social media spaces? Which will you avoid talking about at all?

Any educator working in social media spaces needs to recognize that his or her private life only begins after walking away from the keyboard. Regardless of our intentions, content shared online is instantly permanent, replicable, and available to large audiences.

1. Knowing this, which of your personal interests, hobbies, beliefs, and opinions should you avoid talking about in social media spaces?

2. Is there anything about your personal interests that members of your school community might misinterpret?

Finally, educators working in social media spaces need to consistently maintain professional relationships with parents and students they interact with online.

1. How are the members of your school community currently using social media spaces? How likely are they to find you in the online conversations you join? What sorts of interactions can you anticipate having with these stakeholders?

2. What kinds of behaviors do you think will be important to model for the parents and students you interact with online?

Next Steps

Now that you've thought through the kinds of key decisions and good practices that can help make your work in social media spaces personally rewarding and professionally safe, it's time to plan your next steps, a process that begins by answering the following questions.

1. What is already happening with social media in your district? What trends do you see? Who are the stakeholders? Who shares your vision of what's possible? Who has the time and energy to be your partner in this work? What contacts and resources will you be able to tap into as you move forward?

2. How much time and energy do you have to invest in your efforts to integrate social media spaces into your work? Will your students have to pay in loss of your time and attention? What strains might there be on your professional relationships? What risks could emerge to your professional reputation? Is there an actual dollar cost involved in your plans?

3. How long will it take to build the outcome you envision? How will you measure progress? What intermediary deadlines can you set? What is a logical first step for you to take? When will you take it?

EPILOGUE

The Future of Social Media in Education

For Eric Townsley, principal of South Tama Middle School in Tama, Iowa, social media tools have been an intellectual game changer. "Social media tools have changed the way I learn," he explains. "I've made incredible connections with educators throughout the world on Twitter and am passionate about the quality and depth of the learning that I've done there" (E. Townsley, personal communication, August 29, 2010). Townsley is so convinced that digital connections can influence thinking that he is actively crafting professional development opportunities that incorporate social media tools for his faculty. "I know it will take some of my staff outside of their comfort zone," writes Townsley, "but I also know that pushing my teachers to improve their digital learning habits models what we want our students to do" (E. Townsley, personal communication, August 29, 2010).

Townsley has not completely bought into the idea that social media spaces are silver bullets, though. While he recognizes that increasing numbers of parents, students, and stakeholders are embracing services like Facebook, Twitter, and YouTube—and that businesses are actively building communities in social media spaces—Townsley also realizes that there are real stigmas connected to social media in education. Mass media coverage of cyberbullying and faculty members' inappropriate postings to online forums has led to stakeholders who are not always excited to see the schools they support use social media. "There is a lot of negativity regarding Facebook in education in our area," Townsley explains. "It would take a great shift in culture to change those perceptions, and that makes me a little nervous about using social media tools outside of my building" (E. Townsley, personal communication, August 29, 2010).

Winning public approval of social media in Townsley's district requires shifting perceptions inside principals' offices as well. Current communication patterns—centered around school websites, print memos, long-term relationships with local newspapers, and phone and text-messaging systems—seem to be working well. There are few complaints from parents, and the communities his district serves value accurate information shared traditionally. While Townsley's colleagues are progressive educational thinkers, few have found the time to explore social media services as learners—an important first step toward finding value for tools like Twitter and Facebook in school settings—and all are wrestling with rapidly changing policies outlining the legal ramifications of school-based social media efforts.

Finally, Tama, Iowa, is a rural, economically diverse community. As a result, there is no guarantee that every family will be able to easily access messages posted in social media spaces. That is a real concern for Townsley: "I do not want to make some people feel left out if we were to use Facebook as a communication tool. The information I want out there, I want everyone to be able to access" (E. Townsley, personal communication, August 29, 2010).

Townsley does, however, see each of these social media pitfalls as a possibility worth exploring. He intends to post regular messages about school happenings on a blog and—understanding the importance of visual content in our new media ecology—he has plans to post a series of video newsletters on YouTube. He is also presenting to graduate students in educational leadership on his developing work with social media and may even get to the point where he uses popular services to reach out to South Tama's stakeholders. "I'm really focusing on building relationships with students, parents and staff members," he writes. "Using tools such as Facebook or YouTube would be a good way to do that" (E. Townsley, personal communication, August 29, 2010).

Most of the principals that coauthors Bill, Eric, and Jason work with on a daily basis—in online spaces and in their own schools and districts—share Townsley's pragmatic approach toward social media. They see the potential in new spaces to reinvent our instructional, communication, and professional development practices. They also recognize that social media has currency with young teachers—making services like Facebook and Twitter perfect for building the collective intelligence of a faculty—and can enable real opportunities to change the flow of information in our schools. No longer are messages automatically one-directional: from principal to teacher, from teacher to student, or from school to community. Instead, social media spaces facilitate messaging from teachers to students, from teachers to teachers, from students to students, from students to teachers, from parents to schools, and from schools to outside experts and advocates. These opportunities, generally new to education, increase transparency and encourage deep levels of engagement with all stakeholders.

Concerns over protecting student privacy and controlling negative messages, however, remain at the forefront of most conversations about the role that social media should play in schools. Complicating matters is the ever-changing nature of digital tools. Keeping current with privacy settings, new features, trends, and trouble spots can be an overwhelming task for principals held accountable for the actions of their teachers and students. As social media spaces erase the lines between personal and professional, and as the consequences of social media fumbles become increasingly public and permanent, the stakes of incorporating social media into school plans often exceed the comfort level of many administrators.

Does Social Media Really Have a Future in Schools?

Cautious by nature even when they understand the risks of sitting on the social media sidelines, educators tend to value stability over adopting the kinds of practices that are essential to success in new digital spaces. Instead of being ready to innovate, many teachers, principals, and educational leaders see services like Facebook and Twitter as fads and wonder whether social media spaces really have a future in schools.

Far from a fad, *social computing*—a term used to describe the relationship between social behavior and computer systems that was popularized in James Surowiecki's *The Wisdom of Crowds* (2004)—is likely to grow exponentially in the next decade as more people connect to the web from more places than ever before. David Armano notes that "social networking will be on the go, out of the house, and out of the office. More competition, variety, power, and affordability in devices will fuel the increase of ubiquitous social computing" (Armano, 2010).

Adam Ostrow, author of the blog post "The Next 5 Years in Social Media," echoes Armano's thoughts:

> The next five years are going to see even more dramatic change. Fueled by advancements in underlying technology—the wires, wireless networks and hardware that make social media possible—a world where everything is connected awaits us. The result will be both significant shifts in our everyday lives and a changing of the guard in several industries that are only now starting to feel the impact of social media. (Ostrow, 2010)

Education will be one of those industries that see significant shifts and a changing of the guard as a result of the widespread adoption of social media spaces in the lives of our increasingly connected communities. Parents and teachers who have grown to expect open channels, instant responses, and customized opportunities to participate—and who, increasingly, will have grown up in social media spaces—will lose faith in buildings that refuse to adapt. Instead of hiding from this new media ecology, tomorrow's best principals will embrace the transparency and portability that tools like Twitter and Facebook enable, creating and managing multiple streams of communication at once.

Our classrooms will change, too. No different than their parents—or any motivated learner for that matter—today's students crave opportunities to connect with likeminded individuals. Driven to share their thoughts, ideas, products, and experiences, students will demand classrooms that use social media tools and spaces as gathering points, bringing together peers and potential mentors with similar passions from around the globe. With content readily available everywhere, classrooms will become clearinghouses where students are taught to identify both reliable ideas *and* individuals to learn from. No longer will learning be a lockstep march through a standardized curriculum delivered only inside the walls of a schoolhouse. Instead, as education consultant Tom Vander Ark imagines, social networks will stand at the center of a student's learning universe, providing customized learning experiences that were once unimaginable fantasies:

> Instead of a classroom as the primary organizing principle, social networks will become the primary building block of learning communities (both formal and informal). Smart recommendation engines will queue personalized content. Tutoring, training, and collaboration tools will be applications that run on social networks. New schools will be formed around these capabilities. Teachers in existing schools will adopt free tools yielding viral, bureaucracy-cutting productivity improvement. (Vander Ark, 2009)

Stephen Downes, a senior researcher for Canada's National Research Council, echoes this push toward individualization, "We need, first, to take charge of our own learning, and next, help others take charge of their own learning. We need to move beyond the idea that an education is something that is provided for us, and toward the idea that an education is something that we create for ourselves" (Downes, 2010).

The most important lesson we will be teaching our students, then, is the same lesson Eric Townsley, the principal spotlighted in the introduction of this chapter, learned: networked learning is powerful learning. As Karl Fisch, director of technology at Arapahoe High School in Centennial, Colorado, explains:

> Who you know is what you know. . . . If you have a well-developed, well-nurtured learning network, and you have the access and the skills necessary to utilize it, then you "know" more than someone who does not. You truly have the ability for "just in time" learning. You can reach out to your PLN with a question, with something you want to know more about, and they can help you learn about it. Even if someone in your network isn't an "expert" on the topic, more than likely someone in your network knows someone who is. (Fisch, 2009)

The good news is that the buildup to these kinds of networked learning spaces in schools has been coming for the better part of the past decade. The widespread adoption of popular content management systems like Blackboard (www.blackboard.com) and Moodle (http://moodle.org) that allow teachers to post assignments and resources for students *have* helped to extend classroom walls. The problem is that communication in these systems traditionally remains unidirectional—teachers create, and students consume—and our students want more from their time in and out of the schoolhouse walls. What is needed, and what services like Schoology (www.schoology .com) and Everloop (www.everloop.com) are trying to create, are online environments that blend traditional content-management practices with extended social-networking opportunities for every student, including those in elementary schools. In the best of tomorrow's classrooms, conversations from teacher to student, student to student, student to expert, and teacher to expert will take place anytime, anywhere, and between *anyone* with a connection to the web, creating more opportunities for *everyone* to learn.

Educational institutions are beginning to experiment with all of these practices. Duke University in Durham, North Carolina, recently rolled out a site dedicated to its social media efforts (http://socialmedia.duke.edu). Boarding schools, like Gould Academy in Bethel, Maine, are attracting prospective students using media-rich graphic blogs (http://glog.gouldacademy.org). Individual classes are creating mashups—final products that utilize content from more than one external source—like Worcester Academy's the WA Mash (http://wamash.worcesteracademy.org), and educators are creating sites like edSocialMedia (http://edsocialmedia.com) to create an avenue for others to learn how social media can look in our schools. Drawing from the experiences of increasingly savvy teachers and students, social media spaces will redesign and eventually redefine our concepts of classrooms.

The process will be messy, though. Innovators will push boundaries, finding new applications of social media tools in education that will make many of us uncomfortable. We will be forced to rethink everything we know about schools in order to stay relevant in a world where connected learning in online spaces makes it possible for anyone to learn efficiently without us. We will also have to find a comfortable middle ground between the seemingly radical ideas of those on the cutting edge and the resistance of those committed to traditions (Shirky, 2010).

Ultimately, however, the question is not, "Do social media tools have a future in our schools?" but rather, "How will schools of the future use social media?"

Next Steps

The good news for school leaders is that incorporating social media tools into your professional practices does not have to be intimidating as long as you are willing to tackle a few action steps: build your own network, consult and influence district social media policies, build awareness and gain allies, start with blogs, and grow from the inside out.

Build Your Own Network

As we have recommended in almost every chapter of this book, the first step principals interested in social media spaces should take is to begin building their own personal learning networks with digital tools. Sign up for Twitter, and start following the conversations happening there. Tap into the communities of teachers and principals learning to use social media tools together in places like Classroom 2.0 (www.classroom20.com), the Educator's PLN Ning (http://edupln.ning.com), or the English Companion Ning (http://englishcompanion.ning.com). Doing so is bound to leave you convinced that social media can change the ways that organizations communicate and individuals learn.

Be prepared to feel lost at first, though. Like any new behavior, mastering interactions in social media spaces takes consistent practice. Over time, you will gain a much better feel for why your effort to integrate social media tools into the work of your school makes sense. It is far easier to articulate the strengths—and to imagine the possibilities—of social media spaces as tools for communication and professional development when you are actively using those tools on your own.

Consult and Influence District Social Media Policies

Most principals incorporating social media spaces into their work feel alone at first, seeing little evidence that any other local schools or districts use popular services like Facebook and Twitter. No matter how alone you feel, however, there are active conversations about the role that social media should play in education happening somewhere in your system. That means you should consult the departments responsible for setting digital directions before moving forward with your plans to use social media tools for communication or professional development.

Find out who the influential individuals are. Ask them to explain their core beliefs about the role of social media in education, and then determine whether their positions have been established as official policies. Doing so will help you structure your next steps. If policies have not been established yet, you will have more flexibility to experiment with—and to influence the future direction of—social media use in your district. If clear policies are in place, however, you will have to work within the guidelines as they are currently written.

Build Awareness and Gain Allies

The chances are also good that your questions about using services like Twitter and Facebook to connect with your community or to improve the professional learning in your building are going to be met with initial skepticism. After all, examples of the successful use of social media in education are few and far between. That means you are going to have to build awareness and allies in order to change perceptions in your district.

Start by reading everything you can about social media use in progressive schools and businesses—including the materials shared in the handout "Ten Sources for Learning More About Social Media" (page 75). Connect with other innovative principals, either in person or online, and study how they are using social media in their schools. Figure out what is working. Record things you would like to try. Share survey results demonstrating the need for building a presence in social media spaces. Run budget numbers comparing the costs of reaching out with social media to the costs of more traditional forms of messaging and professional development.

Once you are well versed in exactly what is possible with social media tools in education, start building allies. Find someone in your central office who is willing to experiment with you and to advocate for new policies. Consider reaching out to leaders in the district communications department; they are likely to be the most interested in the ways that social media spaces are changing human interactions. Together, organize and maintain a collection of school-based social media success stories to share. By building awareness one conversation at a time, you can encourage your colleagues to accept the role that social media can play in communication and professional development plans.

Start With Blogs

The most intimidating part of incorporating social media tools into the work of schools is often the fear that negative feedback from stakeholders will dominate online discussions and ruin a school's reputation. If potential disasters—which are entirely possible when social media projects are poorly managed—are preventing positive conversations about the role that social media tools can play in your district, consider using blogs for early communication and professional development work.

While not as dynamic as Twitter and Facebook, blogs are often the safest social media starting point for schools because they allow owners to easily moderate conversations (in comment sections) by monitoring all additions before the general public sees them. As a result, blogs provide many of the advantages of social media tools—ease of publishing, opportunities to transparently share authentic voice, chances for two-way communication—without the perceived risks that come with the kinds of instant, always-on interactions other services enable.

Popular services like Edublogs (http://edublogs.org), WordPress (http://wordpress.com), and Blogger (www.blogger.com) make it easy to establish a blog for communicating with stakeholders, complete with the tools to moderate conversations. Principals interested in using social media to enhance professional development plans can encourage teachers to regularly read popular blogs about teaching and learning and to join in the online conversations happening in the comment sections. Services like Alltop (http://alltop.com) have even created customized pages tracking the thoughts of important education writers (http://education.alltop.com).

Grow From the Inside Out

A final strategy for easing into social media spaces is to grow your work from the inside out. Using private pages on free social-networking services like Facebook or paid services like Ning to connect with faculty members carries few organizational risks. Messages can be shared, features explored, and patterns of interaction mastered before ever inviting broader audiences to join your conversations. Knowing that your initial work with social media tools is happening out of view of the general public should encourage you to develop the authentic, brave, and consistent behaviors necessary for future efforts to succeed.

Don't be afraid to turn over control of your social media spaces to talented young teacher leaders. Not only are they already aware of the kinds of tools that resonate with their peers, their involvement is likely to convince others that your efforts to create meaningful online learning spaces are genuine and authentic. There is nothing in the social media playbook that says the principal has to be both the head coach *and* the starting quarterback!

Let's face it: working to incorporate social media tools into your school's communication and professional development plans will require professional courage and innovation. You are going to have to change behaviors *and* minds. As Don Tapscott (2008), author of *Grown Up Digital: How the Net Generation Is Changing Your World*, writes, "It's much harder to teach old dogs new tricks. Learning a whole new way of communicating, accessing information, and entertaining oneself is hard work, and our established patterns of thinking must change to accommodate the new technology" (Tapscott, 2008, Kindle location 551).

There is no doubt, however, that incorporating social media tools into your school's communication and professional development plans is essential. With 61 percent of all online adults using social-networking tools—a 53 percent jump in just five years, and a percentage that is only going to grow—sharing important messages in places like Facebook and Twitter just makes sense (Madden, 2010; Pew Internet and American Life Project, 2009).

What's more, younger workers are rarely satisfied with accepting the status quo. They almost always expect the kinds of tools that they have embraced for personal communication, collaboration, and learning to be incorporated into their professional lives. They are constantly looking for conversations and frustrated by the dissonance between the instant, collaborative world that they occupy off the clock and the stagnant workplaces they have inherited (Tapscott, 2008). As Moritz Kettler—a young professional spotlighted in Don Tapscott's *Grown Up Digital* (2008)—argues, "Working in a typical company can really sap one's energy because things happen so slowly. There's a big culture clash in the workplace with my generation and the bosses, who can often be much older" (Kindle location 1868–1872).

Most importantly, though, social media tools are redefining the way your students are interacting with one another. In fact, three out of every four online teens are already using services like Facebook, MySpace, and Twitter to stay connected with one another (Lenhart, Purcell, Smith, & Zickuhr, 2010). Isn't it time that we worked to respect, rather than ridicule and ban, the spaces that our students are creating? Wouldn't responsible teaching involve showing students how the social tools they have already embraced can be leveraged for learning—and couldn't experimenting with new spaces for communication and professional development leave you better prepared to find ways to responsibly integrate social media into your building's instructional practices?

Those are the kinds of powerful questions that are waiting for your answers!

Ten Sources for Learning More About Social Media

One of the first steps that principals interested in incorporating social media strategies into their communication and professional development plans should take is to read about the role that new tools are playing in schools and businesses. The following readings and resources are good starting points for initial studies about the changing nature of communication, professional development, and learning in a world that social media spaces dominate.

Websites

There are literally dozens of blogs and websites—many of which were introduced in chapter 2—focusing on the role that social media tools are playing in education. Two in particular, however, are bound to be of value to principals interested in using social media tools for instruction, communication, and professional development.

edSocialMedia

www.edsocialmedia.com

The edSocialMedia website started in 2008 as a home for extending the natural conversations occurring between four friends interested in the role social media was playing in education. Since then, it has become one of the most significant online destinations for educators studying social media in schools. Anchored by a thorough and provocative blog (www.edsocialmedia.com/blog/topic) and offering opportunities for extended learning through social media boot camps, the edSocialMedia community is worth exploring.

Connected Principals

www.connectedprincipals.com

The Connected Principals website is a group blog that twenty different principals serving schools across the demographic spectrum maintain. Writing about topics ranging from best educational practices and distributed leadership to school branding and technology integration, the Connected Principals are generating content that you're bound to find valuable. Be sure to explore the comment section of each entry. Imagine how interactions between blog authors and readers can become a regular part of your school's communication plan.

Books

While there aren't many titles covering the use of social media tools in schools, there have been dozens of great books written for businesses interested in entering social media spaces. Consider the following.

Power Friending: Demystifying Social Media to Grow Your Business

Written by social media expert Amber Mac (2010), *Power Friending* just might be the most approachable explanation of the ins and outs of using social media to connect with communities ever written. Covering the characteristics of successful social media efforts and introducing the basic tools that companies are embracing, *Power Friending* is a great read for any school leader serious about exploring the role social media can play in schools. (Readers interested in listening to Amber Mac talk about social media in education with Steve Hargadon of Classroom 2.0 can visit http://bit.ly/ambermacinterview for a podcast.)

Twitterville: How Businesses Can Thrive in New Global Neighborhoods

Focused specifically on the role that Twitter is playing in 21st century communication patterns, *Twitterville* (Israel, 2009) is an easy read detailing the work of several different individuals and businesses that have used Twitter to authentically engage with the communities to which they are connected. Full of true stories culled from author Shel Israel's interviews during the course of his career as a social media blogger and public speaker, *Twitterville* can help principals understand Twitter, a social media tool that educators often misunderstand.

Grown Up Digital: How the Net Generation Is Changing Your World

Designed as an introduction to the communication patterns and expectations of the Net Generation—individuals between the ages of thirteen and thirty-two—*Grown Up Digital* (Tapscott, 2008) is a must-read for any principal who wants to be responsive to the desires of younger teachers. Covering topics ranging from the way Net Generation brains process information to the kinds of strategies and behaviors businesses can use to recruit, engage, and retain younger workers, author Don Tapscott uses his experiences as the chief executive of a think tank focused on innovation in business to create one of the most useful guides to understanding today's employees.

Twitter Feeds and Diigo Collections

The best places to keep up with the ever-changing social media landscape are online conversations and communities. Consider searching for the following tags and hashtags on Twitter (www.twitter.com) and Diigo (www.diigo.com) to find the latest resources that educators interested in taking advantage of the power of social media in schools are using.

Twitter Hashtag: #cpchat

http://bit.ly/cpchatresults

The principals responsible for the Connected Principals website—and the readers who join them for regular conversations on the role that technology can play in education—use the Twitter hashtag #cpchat to make the resources they are sharing easy to find for other Twitter users. By visiting this link, you can quickly skim the content these leaders are exploring in the effort to make social media a more significant part of the work being done in schools.

Twitter Hashtag: #edchat

http://bit.ly/edchatresults

Many progressive teachers, administrators, and professional development providers interested in joining together to share meaningful resources related to the changing nature of education in the 21st century have adopted the hashtag #edchat. Here, you're guaranteed to find interesting links being shared and questions being asked. You'll also be able to spot like minds that may be worth adding to your personal learning network. Finally, you'll be able to join regular weekly conversations focused on aspects of education ranging from assessment to technology integration.

Twitter Stream: Pew Internet and American Life Project

http://twitter.com/Pew_Internet

The Pew Internet and American Life Project (http://pewinternet.org), a project dedicated to studying the impact that the Internet is having on American society, is the premier provider of research on topics ranging from the social media habits of teens to the ways demographic groups use online resources differently. This link connects to the Twitter stream of the Pew Internet team and is a great place to find direct links to new reports the Pew researchers are publishing.

Diigo Tag: Social Media

www.diigo.com/tag/socialmedia

Diigo, a social bookmarking service that allows users to easily share web finds with one another, has huge collections of current information on social media spaces. This constantly updated link includes every website that Diigo users tag with the label *socialmedia*. While not specifically created for or spotted by educators, the resources included in this collection are current and likely to contain reads that you'll find interesting.

Diigo Tag: Social Networking

www.diigo.com/tag/socialnetworking

Much like the *socialmedia* Diigo tag, this link connects to a constantly updated collection of resources that Diigo users are tagging *socialnetworking*. While the resources included here are not always specifically connected to education, they will keep you connected to the trends in conversations around the role that social media is playing in our lives.

REFERENCES AND RESOURCES

Alexa. (n.d.). About Twitter. Accessed at www.alexa.com/siteinfo/twitter.com on January 5, 2011.

Armano, D. (2010, December 6). Six social media trends for 2011 [Web log post]. Accessed at http://blogs .hbr.org/cs/2010/12/six_social_media_trends_for_20_1.html on January 5, 2011.

Arnold, M., Perry, R., Watson, R., Minatra, K., & Schwartz, R. (2006). *The practitioner: How successful principals lead and influence.* Ypsilanti, MI: National Council of Professors of Educational Administration. Accessed at http://cnx.org/content/m14255/1.1 on January 5, 2011.

Beals, S. R. (2010a, July 28). Superintendent's Facebook posts could be trouble. *Hartford Courant.* Accessed at http://articles.courant.com/2010–07–28/news/hc-windsor-locks -superintendent-0728–20100727_1_superintendent-s-job-new-school-superintendent -social-media on March 3, 2011.

Beals, S. R. (2010b, September 15). Windsor Locks superintendent resigns as part of settlement. *Hartford Courant.* Accessed at http://articles.courant.com/2010–09–15/news/hc-windsor-locks -telesca-0916–20100915_1_facebook-posts-facebook-messages-chairwoman-patricia-king on March 3, 2011.

Beck, L. G., & Murphy, J. (1996). *The four imperatives of a successful school.* Thousand Oaks, CA: SAGE.

boyd, d. (2010). Friendship. In M. Ito, S. Baumer, M. Bittanti, d. boyd, R. Cody, et al., *Hanging out, messing around, and geeking out: Kids living and learning with new media* (pp. 79–115). Cambridge: Massachusetts Institute of Technology.

Browne-Ferrigno, T., & Muth, R. (2004). Leadership mentoring in clinical practice: Role socialization, professional development, and capacity building. *Educational Administration Quarterly, 40*(4), 468–494.

Compete. (2011). *Site profile for twitter.com* [Line graph]. Accessed at http://siteanalytics.compete.com /twitter.com/?metric=uv on January 5, 2011.

Coombs, T. (2008). *Crisis communication and social media.* Gainesville, FL: Institute for Public Relations. Accessed at www.instituteforpr.org/essential_knowledge/detail/crisis_communication_and _social_memed/ on January 5, 2011.

Cross, J. (2007). *Informal learning: Rediscovering the natural pathways that inspire innovation and performance.* San Francisco: Pfeiffer.

Dawson, C. (2011, February 16). Will it ever be time for Facebook? [Web log post]. Accessed at www .zdnet.com/blog/education/will-it-ever-be-time-for-facebook/4498 on February 19, 2011

Digital Buzz Blog. (2010a, March 22). Facebook: Facts and figures for 2010 [Web log post]. Accessed at www.digitalbuzzblog.com/facebook-statistics-facts-figures-for-2010 on January 5, 2011.

Digital Buzz Blog. (2010b, May 12). Infographic: Twitter statistics, facts and figures [Web log post]. Accessed at www.digitalbuzzblog.com/infographic-twitter-statistics-facts-figures on January 5, 2011.

Digital Buzz Blog. (2010c, May 19). Infographic: YouTube statistics, facts and figures [Web log post]. Accessed at www.digitalbuzzblog.com/infographic-youtube-statistics-facts-figures on January 5, 2011.

Dougherty, H. (2010, March 15). Facebook reaches top ranking in US [Web log post]. Accessed at http://weblogs.hitwise.com/heather-dougherty/2010/03/facebook_reaches_top_ranking_i.html on February 20, 2011.

Downes, S. (2010, October 18). A world to change [Web log post]. Accessed at www.huffingtonpost.com /stephen-downes/a-world-to-change_b_762738.html on January 5, 2011.

Drake, T., & Roe, W. (2003). *The principalship* (6th ed.). Columbus, OH: Merrill/Prentice Hall.

Evans, P., & Mohr, N. (1999). Professional development for principals. *Phi Delta Kappan, 80*(7), 530–533.

Fenwick, L., & Pierce, M. (2002). To train or educate: How should the next generation of principals be prepared? *Principal Advisor, 2*(1), 1–2.

Ferriter, B. (2007, April 13). Lessons learned from one fat ox [Web log post]. Accessed at http:// teacherleaders.typepad.com/the_tempered_radical/2007/04/james_surowieck.html on January 5, 2011.

Ferriter, B. (2010a, March 18). Twitter as a tool for professional development [Web log post]. Accessed at http://teacherleaders.typepad.com/the_tempered_radical/2010/03/twitter-as-a-tool-for -professional-development.html on January 5, 2011.

Ferriter, W. M. (2010b). Why teachers should try Twitter. *Educational Leadership, 67*(5), 73–74.

Ferriter, B. (2011a, February 16). Twitter as a social media starting point [Web log post]. Accessed at http://teacherleaders.typepad.com/the_tempered_radical/2011/02/twitter-as-a-social-media -starting-point.html on February 19, 2011.

Ferriter, B. (2011b, February 17). What YOU are saying about social media in schools [Web log post]. Accessed at http://teacherleaders.typepad.com/the_tempered_radical/2011/02/what-you-are -saying-about-social-media-in-schools.html on February 19, 2011.

Fisch, K. (2009, July 22). It's who you know [Web log post]. Accessed at http://thefischbowl.blogspot .com/2009/07/its-who-you-know.html on January 5, 2011.

Foster, E., Loving, C., & Shumate, A. (2000). Effective principals, effective professional development schools. *Teaching and Change, 8*(1), 76–98.

Fox, L. (2010, August 23). Dallas-Fort Worth area schools grapple with social media policies. *Dallas Morning News.* Accessed at www.dallasnews.com/sharedcontent/dws/dn/latestnews/stories /082310dnmetcyberteacher.2a420c1.html on January 5, 2011.

Ganim Barnes, N., & Mattson, E. (2009). *Social media and college admissions: Higher-ed beats business in adoption of new tools for third year.* Dartmouth: University of Massachusetts Dartmouth.

gasstationwithoutpumps. (2011, February 16). Re: Twitter as a social media starting point [Web log post comment]. Accessed at http://teacherleaders.typepad.com/the_tempered_radical/2011/02 /twitter-as-a-social-media-starting-point.html?cid=6a00d8341c721253ef014e5f453547970c #comment-6a00d8341c721253ef014e5f453547970c on February 19, 2011.

Ginsburg, M. (2010, January 4). Fortune 500 companies using social media to reach customers. *Chicago Business.* Accessed at www.chicagobusiness.com/cgi-bin/article.pl?article_id=32875 on January 5, 2011.

Gonzalez, N. (2010, May 23). Check Facebook. Accessed at www.checkfacebook.com on February 20, 2011.

Griffin Good, D., & Kalmon, S. (2010). *Digital learning collaborative: Year 1 report.* Denver, CO: Council on 21st Century Learning. Accessed at http://blogs.stvrain.k12.co.us/instructionaltechnology /files/2010/09/DLCcohort1yr1Rpt061510-final.pdf on September 6, 2010.

Haar, J. M. (2002). *A multiple case study: Principals' involvement in professional development.* Unpublished doctoral dissertation, University of Nebraska–Lincoln. Accessed at http://digitalcommons.unl .edu/dissertations/AAI3041356 on January 5, 2011.

Hampton, K. N., Sessions, L. F., Her, E. J., & Rainie, L. (2009). *Social isolation and new technology: How the Internet and mobile phones impact Americans' social networks.* Washington, DC: Pew Research Center.

Hargadon, S. (2009). *Educational networking: The important role that web 2.0 will play in education.* Pleasanton, CA: Elluminate.

Harris, A. (1998). Effective teaching: A review of the literature. *School Leadership and Management, 18*(2), 169–183.

Heussner, K. M., & Fahmy, D. (2010, August 19). Teacher loses job after commenting about students, parents on Facebook. Accessed at http://abcnews.go.com/Technology/facebook-firing-teacher -loses-job-commenting-students-parents/story?id=11437248&page= on January 5, 2011.

Hoyle, J. R., English, F. W., & Steffy, B. E. (1998). *Skills for successful 21st century school leaders: Standards for peak performers.* Arlington, VA: American Association of School Administrators.

Hui, T. K. (2010, February 16). Religious conflict leads to teacher's suspension. *News and Observer.* Accessed at www.newsobserver.com/2010/02/16/341361/on-facebook-out-of-class.html on January 5, 2011.

ijohnpederson. (2009, April 27). Community building is the new professional development. We forgot that and taught Web 2.0 tools. Discuss [Twitter post]. Accessed at http://favstar.fm/users /ijohnpederson on January 5, 2011.

Israel, S. (2009). *Twitterville: How businesses can thrive in the new global neighborhoods.* New York: Portfolio.

Kostin, M., & Haeger, J. (2006). Coaching schools to sustain improvement [Electronic version]. *The Education Digest, 71*(9), 29–33.

Lairon, M., & Vidales, B. (2003). Leaders learning in context. *Leadership, 32*(5), 16–18, 36.

Lenhart, A. (2010a). *Cyberbullying: What the research is telling us . . . .* Washington, DC: Pew Internet and American Life Project. Accessed at www.slideshare.net/PewInternet/cyberbullying-2010-what -the-research-tells-us-4009451 on January 5, 2011.

Lenhart, A. (2010b). *Social media and young adults.* Washington, DC: Pew Internet and American Life Project. Accessed at http://pewinternet.org/Presentations/2010/Feb/Department-of-Commerce .aspx on January 5, 2011.

Lenhart, A., & Madden, M. (2007). *Social networking websites and teens: An overview.* Washington, DC: Pew Internet and American Life Project.

Lenhart, A., Purcell, K., Smith, A., & Zickuhr, K. (2010). *Social media and young adults.* Washington, DC: Pew Internet and American Life Project.

Li, C., & Bernoff, J. (2008). *Groundswell: Winning in a world transformed by social technologies.* Boston: Harvard Business School Press.

Lipsman, A. (2010, January 5). November sees number of U.S. videos viewed online surpass 30 billion for first time on record [Press release]. *comScore.* Accessed at www.comscore.com/Press_Events /Press_Releases/2010/1/November_Sees_Number_of_U.S._Videos_Viewed_Online_Surpass_30 _Billion_for_First_Time_on_Record on January 5, 2011.

Low-cost laptop could transform learning. (2007, January 2). Accessed at www.msnbc.msn.com /id/16436622/%3E on January 5, 2011.

Lytle, J. (2010, August 16). Facebook the facts: Lee school system sets social media guidelines [Web log post]. Accessed at www.naplesnews.com/blogs/jefflytle/2010/aug/16/schools on January 5, 2011.

Mac, A. (2010). *Power friending: Demystifying social media to grow your business.* New York: Portfolio.

Madden, M. (2010). *Older adults and social media.* Washington, DC: Pew Internet and American Life Project.

Marshall, J. C., Pritchard, R. J., & Gunderson, B. (2001). Professional development: What works and what doesn't. *Principal Leadership, 1*(6), 64–68.

Marzano, R. J., Waters, T., & McNulty, B. A. (2005). *School leadership that works: From research to results.* Alexandria, VA: Association for Supervision and Curriculum Development.

McEwan, E. K. (2003). *Ten traits of highly effective principals: From good to great performance.* Thousand Oaks, CA: SAGE.

McLean, J. (2009, October 19). Technorati State of the Blogosphere 2009: State of the Blogosphere 2009 introduction. Accessed at http://technorati.com/blogging/article/state-of-the-blogosphere-2009 -introduction on January 5, 2011.

Miller, B. M. (2003). *Critical hours: Afterschool programs and educational success.* Quincy, MA: Nellie Mae Education Foundation. Accessed at www.nmefdn.org/uploads/Critical_Hours.pdf on January 5, 2011.

n.a. (2009, December 28). User content creation around the world. *eMarketer: Digital Intelligence.* Accessed at www.emarketer.com/Article.aspx?R=1007440 on January 5, 2011.

n.a. (2010, April 7). Utah school district unveils new teacher web rules. *eSchool News.* Accessed at www .eschoolnews.com/2010/04/07/utah-school-district-unveils-new-teacher-web-rules on January 5, 2011.

National School Boards Association. (2007). *Creating and connecting: Research and guidelines on online social—and educational—networking.* Alexandria, VA: Author. Accessed at www.nsba.org/site /docs/41400/41340.pdf on January 5, 2011.

Nielsenwire. (2010, May 4). Facebook and Twitter post large year over year gains in unique users [Web log post]. Accessed at http://blog.nielsen.com/nielsenwire/global/facebook-and-twitter-post-large -year-over-year-gains-in-unique-users on January 5, 2011.

O'Dell, J. (2010, November 19). Facebook accounts for 25% of all U.S. pageviews. Accessed at http:// mashable.com/2010/11/19/facebook-traffic-stats on February 20, 2011.

Ostrow, A. (2010, September 7). The next five years in social media [Web log post]. Accessed at http:// mashable.com/2010/09/07/next-5-years-social-media on January 5, 2011.

Peacock, M. (2010, July 7). Why social media marketing matters [Web log post]. Accessed at www .edsocialmedia.com/2010/07/why-social-media-marketing-matters on January 5, 2011.

Peterson, K. (2002). The professional development of principals: Innovations and opportunities. *Educational Administration Quarterly, 38*(2), 213–232.

Peterson, K., & Cosner, S. (2005). Teaching your principal. *Journal of Staff Development, 26*(2), 28–32.

Petzko, V. (2004). Tailoring professional development for a better fit. *Principal Leadership, 5*(3), 16–21.

Pew Internet and American Life Project. (2009). *Adults on social network sites, 2005–2009.* Washington, DC: Author. Accessed at www.pewinternet.org/Infographics/Growth-in-Adult-SNS-Use-20052009.aspx on January 5, 2011.

Pew Internet and American Life Project. (2010). *Teen and young adult Internet use.* Washington, DC: Author. Accessed at http://pewresearch.org/millennials/teen-internet-use-graphic.php on January 5, 2011.

Portin, B., Schneider, P., DeArmond, M., & Gundlach, L. (2003). *Making sense of leading schools: A study of the school principalship.* Seattle, WA: Center on Reinventing Public Education. Accessed at http:// mymassp.com/resourcesforprincipals/pdf/makingsense.pdf on January 5, 2011.

Ramsden, J. (2009, May 21). Rocks, diamonds, pearls, and gold; knowledge mining with social media [Web log post]. Accessed at www.jasonramsden.com/home/index.php/myblog/54-knowledge-mining on January 5, 2011.

Ramsden, J. (2010, April 19). Social media perception [Web log post]. Accessed at www.jasonramsden .com/home/index.php/myblog/80-social-media-perception on February 19, 2011.

Sheninger, E. (2010a, March 24). Ideas to increase parent communication in schools [Web log post]. Accessed at http://esheninger.blogspot.com/2010/03/ideas-to-increase-parent-communication .html on January 5, 2011.

Sheninger, E. (2010b, April 22). Reflecting on the 140 conference [Web log post]. Accessed at http:// esheninger.blogspot.com/2010/04/reflecting-on-140-conference_22.html on January 5, 2011.

Sheninger, E. (2010c, August 2). We have got to do and be better [Web log post]. Accessed at http:// esheninger.blogspot.com/2010/08/we-have-got-to-do-and-be-better.html on January 5, 2011.

Sheninger, E. (2010d, August 6). Building momentum [Web log post]. Accessed at http://esheninger .blogspot.com/2010/08/building-momentum.html on January 5, 2011.

Sheninger, E. (2010e, November 1). Opening minds on social networking [Web log post]. Accessed at http://esheninger.blogspot.com/2010/11/opening-minds-on-social-networking.html on January 5, 2011.

Shirky, C. (2010). *Cognitive surplus: Creativity and sharing in a connected age.* New York: Penguin Press.

Stansbury, M. (2009, April 16). Survey shows barriers to Web 2.0 in schools. *eSchool News: Technology News for Today's K–20 Educator.* Accessed at www.eschoolnews.com/2009/04/16/survey-shows-barriers -to-web-2–0-in-schools on February 20, 2011.

Statistics. (n.d.). In *Facebook* [Press Room]. Accessed at www.facebook.com/press/info.php?statistics on January 5, 2011.

Strong, J. H., Richard, H. B., & Catano, N. (2008). *Qualities of effective principals.* Alexandria, VA: Association for Supervision and Curriculum Development.

Surowiecki, J. (2004). *The wisdom of crowds: Why the many are smarter than the few and how collective wisdom shapes business, economies, societies and nations.* New York: Random House.

Tapscott, D. (2008). *Grown up digital: How the net generation is changing your world.* Columbus, OH: McGraw-Hill.

Vander Ark, T. (2009, November 7). How social networking will transform learning. *Huffington Post Education.* Accessed at www.huffingtonpost.com/tom-vander-ark/how-social-networking -wit_b_349467.html on February 19, 2011.

Van Grove, J. (2010, April 20). What social media users want (STATS) [Web log post]. Accessed at http:// mashable.com/2010/03/18/social-media-sites-data/ on January 5, 2011.

Webster, T. (2010). *Twitter usage in America: 2010.* Somerville, NJ: Edison Research.

Weil, K. (2010, February 22). Measuring tweets [Web log post]. Accessed at http://blog.twitter.com/2010 /02/measuring-tweets.html on January 5, 2011.

Whitehurst, G. J. (2009). *Don't forget curriculum.* Washington, DC: Brookings. Accessed at www.brookings .edu/papers/2009/1014_curriculum_whitehurst.aspx on January 5, 2011.

York-Barr, J., Sommers, W. A., Ghere, G. S., & Montie, J. K. (2006). *Reflective practice to improve schools: An action guide for educators* (2nd ed.). Thousand Oaks, CA: Corwin Press.

Zepeda, S. J., Bengtson, E., Parylo, O., Teitelbaum, D., & Shorner-Johnson, K. (2008). *Executive summary: PreK–12 principals—Issues in evaluation, professional development, and succession.* Atlanta, GA: Georgia's Leadership Institute for School Improvement. Accessed at www.galeaders.org/site /default.html on August 1, 2008.

INDEX

Teaching the iGeneration
William M. Ferriter and Adam Garry
Find the natural overlap between the work you already believe in and the digital tools that define tomorrow's learning. Each chapter introduces an enduring skill: information fluency, persuasion, communication, collaboration, and problem solving. Then, the authors present a digital solution that can be used to enhance traditional skill-based instructional practices. A collection of handouts and supporting materials tailored to each skill and tool type ends each chapter.
BKF393

Mobile Learning Devices
Kipp D. Rogers
This brief guide explains why mobile learning is transforming education and how devices such as cell phones can enhance learning in 21st century classrooms. The author provides guidelines principals can use to help staff introduce mobile learning devices into instruction in ways that are safe, engaging, aligned with National Educational Technology Standards, and targeted to promote student learning.
BKF445

What Principals Need to Know About the Basics of Creating Brain-Compatible Classrooms
David A. Sousa
Understand the basics for creating a brain-compatible classroom with this brief, accessible guide customized for principals. This book provides an overview of educational neuroscience designed to help principals construct meaningful professional development that enhances teachers' knowledge and skills about brain-compatible learning.
BKF463

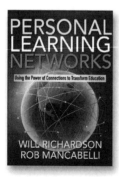

Personal Learning Networks
Will Richardson and Rob Mancabelli
The Internet connects us in unprecedented ways. To prepare students to flourish in this new learning world, schools will need to transform themselves in important ways. This book is a road map for any educator thinking about using the web for learning. Build your own learning network, and use learning networks in the classroom and schoolwide to improve student outcomes.
BKF484

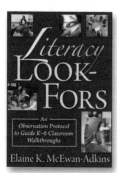

Literacy Look-Fors
Elaine K. McEwan-Adkins
Through the unique seven-step process outlined in *Literacy Look-Fors*, administrators and literacy leaders will gain a solid understanding of how to assess and build instructional capacity, overcome roadblocks, develop professional growth opportunities, and create a balanced literacy program. Learn how to identify the look-fors that provide evidence of effective literacy instruction, and bring all students to grade level or well above.
BKF422

Solution Tree | Press

a division of
Solution Tree

Visit solution-tree.com or call 800.733.6786 to order.

Solution Tree

Solution Tree's mission is to advance the work of our authors. By working with the best researchers and educators worldwide, we strive to be the premier provider of innovative publishing, in-demand events, and inspired professional development designed to transform education to ensure that all students learn.

The mission of the National Association of Elementary School Principals is to lead in the advocacy and support for elementary and middle level principals and other education leaders in their commitment for all children.